How to Find Temporary Work Abroad

In this Series

How to Apply for a Job
How to Apply to an Industrial Tribunal
How to Be a Freelance Secretary
How to Be a Local Councillor
How to Be an Effective School Governor
How to Buy & Run a Shop
How to Buy & Run a Small Hotel
How to Choose a Private School
How to Claim State Benefits
How to Communicate at Work
How to Conduct Staff Appraisals
How to Do Your Own Advertising
How to Emigrate
How to Employ & Manage Staff
How to Enjoy Retirement
How to Find Temporary Work Abroad
How to Get a Job Abroad
How to Get a Job in America
How to Get a Job in Australia
How to Get a Job in Europe
How to Get a Job in France
How to Get a Job in Hotels & Catering
How to Get a Job in Travel & Tourism
How to Get into Films & TV
How to Get That Job
How to Help Your Child at School
How to Invest in Stocks & Shares
How to Keep Business Accounts
How to Know Your Rights at Work
How to Know Your Rights: Students
How to Know Your Rights: Teachers
How to Live & Work in America
How to Live & Work in Australia
How to Live & Work in Belgium
How to Live & Work in France
How to Live & Work in Germany
How to Live & Work in Hong Kong
How to Live & Work in Italy
How to Live & Work in Japan
How to Live & Work in New Zealand
How to Live & Work in Portugal
How to Live & Work in Saudi Arabia
How to Live & Work in Spain
How to Lose Weight & Keep Fit
How to Make a Wedding Speech
How to Manage a Sales Team
How to Manage Budgets & Cash Flows
How to Manage Computers at Work
How to Manage People at Work
How to Manage Your Career
How to Master Book-Keeping
How to Master Business English
How to Master GCSE Accounts
How to Master Languages
How to Master Public Speaking
How to Pass Exams Without Anxiety
How to Pass That Interview
How to Plan a Wedding
How to Prepare Your Child for School
How to Publish a Book
How to Publish a Newsletter
How to Raise Business Finance
How to Raise Funds & Sponsorship
How to Rent & Buy Property in France
How to Rent & Buy Property in Italy
How to Retire Abroad
How to Run a Local Campaign
How to Sell Your Business
How to Spend a Year Abroad
How to Start a Business from Home
How to Start a New Career
How to Study Abroad
How to Study & Live in Britain
How to Survive at College
How to Survive Divorce
How to Take Care of Your Heart
How to Teach Abroad
How to Understand Finance at Work
How to Use a Library
How to Work from Home
How to Work in an Office
How to Write a Report
How to Write a Press Release
How to Write an Assignment
How to Write an Essay
How to Write Business Letters
How to Write for Publication
How to Write for Television

Other titles in preparation

FIND TEMPORARY WORK ABROAD

A world of opportunities for everyone

Nick Vandome

How To Books

By the same author

How to Get a Job in Australia
How to Spend a Year Abroad

British Library Cataloguing in Publication Data
A catalogue record for this book is available from the British Library.

First published in 1994 by How To Books Ltd, Plymbridge House, Estover Road, Plymouth PL6 7PZ, United Kingdom. Tel: (0752) 735251/695745. Fax: (0752) 695699. Telex: 45635.

Note: The material contained in this book is set out in good faith for general guidance and no liability can be accepted for loss or expense incurred as a result of relying in particular circumstances on statements made in the book. The laws and regulations are complex and liable to change, and readers should check the current position with the relevant authorities before making personal arrangements.

Typeset by PDQ Typesetting, Stoke-on-Trent
Printed and bound by BPC Wheatons Ltd, Exeter.

Contents

List of illustrations 6

Preface 7

1 The first step 9

Why look for temporary work abroad? 9
What are the benefits? 12
Economic factors to consider 14
Motivating yourself 16

2 Getting set 18

Obtaining a passport 18
Will you need a visa? 19
Will you need a work permit? 19
Obtaining insurance 20
Taking health precautions 21
Preparing yourself for job hunting 25
Dos and don'ts before you go 26
Checklist 27

3 Achieving high employability 28

Finding sources of information 28
What type of work suits you? 32
What type of work is available? 32
Getting experience before you go 33
Selling yourself before you go 35
Ten steps to finding work before you go 42

4 Areas of temporary employment abroad 43

Joining adventure travel companies 43
Camping firms 44
Ski resort companies 46

Teaching English as a foreign language 47
Voluntary organisations 51
Work camps 60
Working for youth organisations 61

5 The world at a glance 66
Europe 67
Australasia 117
Middle East 127
North America 130
South and Central America 135
Africa 138
Asia 141
The Caribbean 145

6 The final edge 147
Case histories 147

Useful addresses 151

Further reading 153

Index 157

LIST OF ILLUSTRATIONS

1 Acceptable letter of application 37
2 Sample CV 39
3 Map of the world 68
4 Map of Europe 72
5 Map of Spain and Portugal 112
6 Map of Australia 120
7 Map of the USA 132

Preface

Is working abroad for a limited period of time the chance to expand your horizons or a way of subsidising an extended holiday? Well, both really, and a lot more besides. Due to changing attitudes, and also changing economic circumstances, the idea of a temporary job abroad is one that is appealing to a wider range of people than ever before. From school-leavers to university graduates, and middle-aged teachers to unemployed civil servants the prospect of a temporary job abroad is fast becoming a realistic proposition rather than 'something that other people do'.

The variety of work available to the casual worker is as diverse as the countries in which it is offered. The traditional temporary jobs such as fruit-picking and working in the hospitality industry are now supplemented by jobs as various as building dams in southern Africa and modelling contact lenses in Asia. No one should reject the idea of a temporary job abroad on the grounds that there is nothing they fancy on offer — the temporary job menu is a rich and varied one.

Whether we like it or not economics is now playing a large part in the working abroad puzzle. On the home front high unemployment means that there are an increasing number of people who are thinking of a job abroad as an alternative to life on the dole in the UK. However, the other side of this coin is that the worldwide recession has made jobs harder to find everywhere. This should not deter anyone but it does mean that people have to be well prepared for confronting the temporary job market. This book aims to provide some of the information needed to successfully find casual work abroad.

In general terms there are two distinct ways to go about finding a temporary job abroad. The first is to apply to an organisation that specialises in this area, such as a voluntary organisation (voluntary work should be thought of as a very serious option for people wishing to work in a challenging environment), a camping firm or a youth organisation.

The second way to find a job abroad is to pack your bags and look for work as you are travelling. This is not quite as easy as it sounds and you need to put in a certain amount of groundwork to ensure that you do not return home, penniless, within the first week. Organisation and planning ahead are indispensable qualities for someone with this option in mind.

I would like to thank family and friends who have helped with this book and encouraged me along the way. Also grateful thanks go out to all the temporary workers who have offered their opinions and given me pieces of invaluable advice. Anyone who wants to add their own opinions please write to me, c/o How To Books, Plymbridge House, Estover Road, Plymouth PL6 7PZ.

Finally, it should be noted that the temporary-jobs-abroad-creature is one of the least prejudiced beings on this earth — it accepts anyone, regardless of age, race, sex, colour of hair or preference for wearing loud beach shirts.

Nick Vandome

1
The First Step

Although a temporary job abroad is not as major a commitment as a year abroad it is nevertheless a significant step. Since it is something available to anyone, regardless of sex, age or work experience, it cannot be pigeon-holed for one particular section of society. Having said that, different people will have different reasons and motivations for seeking a temporary job abroad.

WHY LOOK FOR TEMPORARY WORK ABROAD?

School-leavers' reasons

For school-leavers going on to further education the reasons for working abroad for a short period of time are evident: it provides a break before undertaking more study, it gives young people a taste of the real world and it gives them work experience which may be invaluable in years to come.

But for youngsters who do not go on to further education a temporary job abroad can be just as important, if not more so. The transition from school into employment or training is far from easy, particularly at a time when teenagers are coming to terms with many other changes in their lives. It is a huge change in lifestyle and the more conservative may say that it is not a good time to thrust a school-leaver into an unusual environment. But why not? Young people are probably more responsive to new ideas and influences, and a brief period of employment abroad may be just what they need to broaden their horizons and maybe readjust their outlook on life.

One of the great advantages of a temporary job abroad for school-leavers is that it can challenge the accepted values with which people have grown up, without being a long-term departure from home. Armed with this experience most people will be better prepared to tackle the trials and tribulations that the real world will throw at them.

Students' and graduates' reasons

Traditionally students are one section of society who consistently indulge in temporary jobs abroad. While studying it can be a way of subsidising summer vacations abroad without having to go grovelling to the bank manager. Then, after three or four years of burning the midnight oil and wearing out library seats it is a way of clearing out the cobwebs before settling down to life as an accountant or a doctor.

However, the cold hand of recession has not ignored the student population. With increasing unemployment among university and college graduates, running at approximately 10%, a period of work abroad is no longer just an alternative form of employment — sometimes it is the only form of employment. If students cannot find a job once they graduate, or are working in a job which they feel is not utilising their degree properly, then the idea of a temporary job abroad should be given serious consideration. It may mean washing dishes in Austria or sweeping streets in Holland but, if nothing else, it means you will not be part of the ever-increasing academic dole queue in the UK.

Reasons for those made redundant

Unfortunately, unemployment and redundancy is becoming a regular part of life in Britain. For many people who lose their jobs there is a feeling of despair that blanks out all alternatives other than trying to get another job as soon as possible. Even if there are no immediate employment prospects there could be a light at the end of the tunnel in the form of a brief sojourn overseas to work.

If someone has lost their job and has received a redundancy payment then it may be worth considering using some of it to finance a period of work abroad. More prudent advice may be to keep the money to cushion you against a prolonged period of unemployment, but conversely it may be more beneficial for your self-esteem to be doing something positive. Also, it is not a holiday you are going on and if you manage to find work then you may come back with more money than when you left. This, and the experience you will have gained, may be thought of as a useful investment.

Obviously this course of action would not be ideal for everyone, particularly someone with a family and financial commitments. But, if you have no strings and you fancy a break from the drudgery of the dole offices, then a temporary job abroad should not be dismissed. It may even be beneficial when you come back and start looking for another job.

Long-term unemployed's reasons

With over a million people who have been unemployed for over a year it would be facile to suggest that a simple solution to the problem is for everyone to pack their bags and go and pick fruit in France or work in a hotel in Spain. The most glaring obstacle to this would be the lack of money and many people would simply not have the resources to travel abroad.

However, people who have been out of work for an extended period should not automatically feel that a temporary job abroad is not for them. Perhaps most importantly, the very idea could give people a focus in their lives, rather than the daily disappointment of facing closed doors. Researching and planning a project of this nature can provide optimism, enthusiasm and a fresh outlook on life. There is nothing worse than facing a dead-end future and a temporary job abroad can provide the slip-road to better days.

Money is still a major consideration but if someone is determined to do something like this then the 'where there's a will there's a way' cliché comes into play. Borrow a tent and a backpack, exercise your thumb and hitchhike to Europe and begin looking for a job there. It may not be an ideal situation but neither is being part of Britain's unemployed.

One other factor to consider about unemployment — it is not a creation over which Britain has an exclusive copyright. If we are to believe the politicians the recession is a worldwide phenomenon, not just a British one. People should not think that because they cannot find a job here then the streets of various countries abroad will be paved with employment. Being unemployed in Australia is no more exotic than being unemployed in Britain so make sure you know what type of employment environment you are heading towards.

Taking a short-term break

Doctors picking fruit for a month in Germany; school teachers teaching English in Thailand during summer holidays; civil servants crewing on a yacht in the Mediterranean; and bar managers waiting on tables on the Cost Del Sunshine. Temporary jobs abroad can be taken by people in steady jobs at home. If the desire to do it is strong then it should be done: security is nice but life is short. Security counts for little when you compare it to unfulfilled dreams.

Taking a working holiday

For many people with a dose of wanderlust the finances and the desired location do not always equate. This is where a temporary job can come to the rescue. Many people follow a temporary job 'circuit', working for a few weeks in one area and then moving on to the next. This is particularly true of those in seasonal work such as fruit-picking and tourism. This can be the ideal way to finance a holiday that otherwise may have been out of reach.

If the idea of a working holiday appeals to you then find out where the work is first and then plan your holiday arrangements around that. If you do it the other way around then you may discover that there is not as much temporary work in Afghanistan or Burma as you had first hoped.

WHAT ARE THE BENEFITS?

Increasing your self-confidence

It sounds obvious to say that you will become a more well-rounded person by working in an unfamiliar country but the influence of this type of experience cannot be overstressed. Freed from the conventions and shackles of 'doing what is expected' people working abroad have the opportunity to express themselves in the way they want to rather than the way they think they should. None of us know everything about ourselves but by testing yourself in this way you will discover sides of your character that even you did not know you possessed.

The thought of starting a new job in a strange country is daunting by any standards but if you have the courage to take the plunge then the rewards will probably last you a lifetime. When you return home after working abroad, even for a few weeks, you will notice how your values have changed: is it really earth-shatteringly important to wash the car at 3.45 pm every Sunday? Does it matter if the washing-up gets left overnight? Will the world come to an end if the answering machine does not get switched on every time you leave the house?

Working abroad may challenge every prejudice and belief that you hold — but then life would be mind-numbingly dull if we were never challenged.

Obtaining greater work experience

As unemployment can be the motivation for looking for a temporary job abroad in the first place, then finding a job on your return should also be on the agenda. While working abroad may not provide you with a folder full of references with which to dazzle personnel managers at ICI or IBM it will give you the chance to do something different, and this in itself can be put to good use when you return home. You could approach prospective employers with the following attributes:

- Ability to work under your own initiative — travelling overseas and finding a job could impress even the most hardened personnel manager.

- Flexibility — if you can work in a variety of jobs abroad then you may convince prospective employers that you will be able to do anything that they ask.

- Ability to get on with people — most employers are anxious to employ people who will get on well with their fellow workers. If you can do this while working abroad then you should emphasise this factor when you are looking for work at home.

When you have returned home and you are applying for a job it is important to stress that you have not been 'lazing around'. Unfortunately, some employers seem to equate a period of short-term employment abroad with instability and a peripatetic nature. Your task will be to stress the numerous advantages of your period of employment abroad and also to convince them that you are not going to disappear abroad again at the drop of a work permit. Brush up on your sales technique — present your time abroad as a strategic career move that will give you a distinct advantage over the other candidates.

Being active and positive

Even if the worst comes to the worst and you have a terrible experience working abroad then your time will not have been wasted — if nothing else you will have discovered that a job abroad is perhaps not for you. But two of the most important benefits from the experience, whether it is good or bad, are:

- You are keeping busy rather than sitting at home watching the grass grow.

- You are trying to make things happen rather than waiting for a fairy godmother to endow you with wealth and success.

The positive effects of working abroad cannot be stressed strongly enough. Not only will you be working but you will also be dealing with other challenges such as a different language and a different culture. Once this has been tackled it tends to cultivate an even more positive attitude — and so it goes on until you are prepared to tackle anything. This may seem unlikely as you contemplate your immediate future from the security of your home but many people have returned from working abroad with a much more positive and enthusiastic attitude than when they left.

Widening your horizons

The days of large swaths of pink dominating the world atlas have long since passed and Britain's and other dominating countries' influences have been greatly reduced. This has led to countries all around the world asserting their own culture and heritage. To people used to our rather staid British ways this can be something of a major revelation.

What do Spanish workers do during their lunch hours? Where do Japanese workers socialise? What do Australians consider a hard day's graft? Where does the work ethic come in the scheme of things in South Africa? The answers to all of these questions may be found when you undertake a period of employment abroad. Even what may seem like obvious points will provide important insights into a country's psyche. A period of working abroad not only opens eyes, it also opens minds.

ECONOMIC FACTORS TO CONSIDER

How much money should I take?

This will vary on where you hope to work — obviously you will need a few more pennies if you are going to Australia rather than France — but a reasonable way to calculate what you will need is to work out your expenses (travel, accommodation, food) and then double it. This is because travelling abroad in any form is a bit like a night out on the town: however much you think you will need you always end up with empty pockets and have to go to an autobank to pay the taxi-driver.

Since the idea is to work when you get to your destination the amount of money that you will need will not be as much as for an outright holiday. However, there are a few points that you should consider as far as money and employment are concerned:

- You may be working for low wages and so need to supplement your income.

- When you find a job you may need to pay for accommodation/ clothes/equipment.

- Just as at home, there are always unforeseen expenses that creep up behind you and hit you over the back of the head with an empty wallet.

- 'Murphy's Law of Employment' — when you are most in need of money you will lose your job.

Despite the desirability to take as much money as possible this does not mean that you have to stay at home just because of a lack of cash — as far as the temporary job world is concerned: 'Where there's a will there's a pay-packet waiting somewhere'. It may take a bit more initiative to get yourself to your destination but initiative is a commodity that all temporary workers should pack in considerable quantities.

Will the recession affect you?

As the politicians often tell us, the recession in Britain is the result of a wider, more far-reaching recession that encompasses most of the western world. This being the case it would be less than optimistic to hope that it will be easier to find employment abroad than it is at home. However, things are not as bleak as they may at first seem — the temporary job-seeker tends to be more recession-proof than his or her more high-flying counterpart.

While the recession is having a notable effect on business and industry around the world it is unlikely that the temporary worker will want to become a businessman/woman or an industrialist. If you are looking for a long-term, permanent job abroad then 'recession' may loom large on your horizons. But if you are looking for temporary work then it will have less effect. There will always be a need for bar staff, hotel workers, fruit pickers, au pairs, farm-hands and labourers, although you may find that there are more people chasing each vacancy.

Although the world recession has not made it any easier for the temporary worker it is not the monster that some people would have us believe.

Improving your prospects

Before setting foot from the sanctuary of home you should do some preliminary work on the task ahead.

- Find out as much general information as possible about the countries in which you want to work.

- Decide what type of work you want to do.
- Ask yourself what qualities or qualifications you have to do this type of work.
- If you feel you do not have the suitable qualifications, do something about it! This could include nightclasses, part-time work or voluntary work.
- Speak to people who have worked abroad as there is nothing to beat personal experience. Universities or colleges are a good place to start looking.
- Get in touch with organisations who deal with temporary jobs abroad and ask them if they can put you in touch with people who have worked overseas.
- Buy this book and tell all your temporary-job-seeking friends to do the same.

What will you miss at home?

One of the greatest fears of people who undertake temporary work abroad is that they will have been left behind when they return home. School-leavers think their friends will already be busy working or studying; graduates feel the job market will have passed them by; and people who are looking for work think they may be branded unreliable.

While these are all valid fears, one of the joys of a temporary job abroad is that it is just that – a period of a few weeks or months. It is amazing how little can happen at home during that time and the experiences gained from a period of employment abroad will easily outweigh any slight disadvantages. Any lost ground can quickly be regained and employers should look at time abroad as a distinct benefit and treat your CV accordingly.

MOTIVATING YOURSELF

Ten positive steps

1. Remember that the daily routine of your life will still be there when you return — if you want it back.

2. Think of unusual occupations in different countries — and accept that you could be part of that.

3. Be aware of the pitfalls and tackle them head on rather than avoid them.

4. Ask a friend to keep doing your pools coupon — just in case.

5. Remember to have the milk and the newspapers cancelled.

6. Ask yourself 'Is my current job really so important?'

7. Make sure you have enough money to propel you to your destination.

8. Prepare yourself for the fact that you are going to experience a totally different way of life — keep an open mind about the prospect.

9. List the advantages you will have gained once you return.

10. Remember to arrange for pets to be cared for.

2
Getting Set

Before you take your first job-seeking step on foreign soil there are a number of areas that you need to look into very carefully:

- passport
- insurance
- visas
- work permits
- health

Look at these as the foundations of your temporary-job-abroad-home. If the foundations are not secure then the whole structure may collapse like a skyscraper in quicksand.

OBTAINING A PASSPORT

Everyone knows you need a passport to travel overseas but it is surprising how many people leave it to the last minute to apply for one, or suddenly realise that it will run out halfway through their trip. Even if your passport is valid until after your proposed date of return it may be necessary to apply for a new one: some countries, including Australia and Thailand, require a passport to be valid for a period of time beyond the length of your intended stay. This varies from three to six months but to be on the safe side it is best to have twelve months leeway.

It is a good idea to memorise your passport number — it will save you a lot of time while filling in visa forms and suchlike.

Passport offices in the UK

- London Passport Office, Clive House, 70 Petty France, London SW1H 9HD. Tel: (071) 279 3434.

- Liverpool Passport Office, 5th Floor, India Buildings, Water Street, Liverpool L2 0QZ. Tel: (051) 237 3010.

- Newport Passport Office, Olympia House, Upper Dock Street, Newport, Gwent NP9 1XA. Tel: (0633) 244500.

- Peterborough Passport Office, Aragon Court, Northminster Road, Peterborough, Cambs PE1 1QG. Tel: (0733) 894445.

- Glasgow Passport Office, 3 Northgate, 96 Milton Street, Cowcaddens, Glasgow G4 0BT. Tel: (041) 332 0271.

- Belfast Passport Office, Hampton House, 47–53 High Street, Belfast BT1 2QS. Tel: (0232) 232371.

Make sure you apply for your passport in good time — months, rather than weeks, before your departure. Processing of your application will take longer over Christmas and at the height of summer.

WILL YOU NEED A VISA?

Visas are the magical stamps in your passport which allow you to enter and leave foreign countries. Although you do not need them for EC member states (and in some instances the USA and certain Eastern Bloc countries) you will for most other countries. Visas invariably cost money so you will have to include this in your travel budget.

Where to get them

In Britain visas are issued from foreign embassies, most of which are located in London. Visas can also be obtained as you are travelling but you must have one before you can enter that particular country.

WILL YOU NEED A WORK PERMIT?

As with visas some countries require you to have a permit enabling you to work in their country. See Chapter 5 for countries where a work permit is not required for residents of the UK — these are mostly fellow members of the EC. Before considering temporary work in a particular country write to the relevant embassy asking for details of how to apply for a work permit, if applicable.

In some countries you can only get a work permit if you are taking up a permanent job that has been arranged before you arrive.

This is designed to ensure that jobs in that country are offered to their own citizens where possible.

For the temporary worker work permits may appear to be a major stumbling block. There is the option of working without one, although in some countries this will not be possible because there is no work available, and it is possible to find temporary work while travelling on a visitor's visa, but this is illegal, and therefore not recommended. It is up to individuals to decide whether they want to take the risk. People do work without work permits — it is a case of 'you pay your money and you take your choice'.

OBTAINING INSURANCE

Insurance may seem like an expensive luxury, but it is not — it is an absolute necessity, as was shown recently by a couple who went on holiday to America. The woman was seven months pregnant but she unexpectedly had the baby prematurely while on holiday. The hospital bill came to £80,000 and her husband said that the couple of hundred pounds they paid on insurance was the best investment they had ever made.

Available cover

These are some areas you should have on your insurance policy.

Medical expenses

This is the most important part of your insurance policy and you should not set foot overseas if you do not have this. The range of cover varies but a minimum of £250,000 would be recommended while a sum of £1 million should be considered seriously, especially if you are going to be travelling in North America where medical insurance can, quite literally, be bankrupting.

Personal accident

This allows for the payment of a lump sum to the policyholder in the event of an accident, such as the loss of a finger or serious disablement. The sum varies depending on the injury and most policies have fixed amounts.

Loss of baggage and money

It is a good idea to be insured against the loss of your belongings and your money.

Personal liability

This insures you against sums payable if someone decides to sue you for injury, loss or damage to other people or their property.

Cancellation

If the policyholder has to cancel a journey for a genuine reason such as ill health then any money already paid as a deposit is covered.

Strikes and delays

This means you are compensated if your journey (from Britain) is delayed or affected by a strike.

Travel insurance companies

- Automobile Association, Fanum House, Leicester Square, London W1. Tel: (0345) 500600. Provide cover for overland travel abroad.

- Campbell Irvine Ltd, 48 Earls Court Road, Kensington, London W8 6EJ. Tel: (071) 937 6981. Offer personal and vehicle insurance.

- Hanover Insurance Brokers, 80–86 Westow Street, Upper Norwood SE19 3AF. Tel: (081) 771 8844. Offer personal and extensive vehicle insurance.

- International Student Insurance Service. Available from Endsleigh Insurance Services Ltd, Endsleigh House, Ambrose Street, Cheltenham Spa, Gloucester GL50 3NR. Good all-round travel insurance policies at very competitive prices.

- WEXAS International, 45–49 Brompton Road, London SW3 1DE. Tel: (071) 589 0500. Offer members comprehensive insurance at very competitive prices.

TAKING HEALTH PRECAUTIONS

Being sick overseas can be a very demoralising experience. At best you will be in considerable discomfort for a few days or weeks and at worst you will have to come home, thus wrecking your plans. While it is impossible to guard totally against illness there are a number of precautions you can take.

Vaccinations

When travelling abroad to certain countries some vaccinations are essential while for others they are strongly recommended.

Yellow fever and cholera

Under international health regulations yellow fever and cholera certificates are required for parts of Africa and South America.

Poliomyelitis (polio)

Although most people in Britain will have been vaccinated against it you may need a booster. These should be every five years for travellers.

Rabies

Prevalent in rural Africa, Asia and South America, but also common in parts of Europe. Vaccinations can be given before you go but these are generally reserved for people who will be working with animals. Rabies is fatal if it is not treated immediately. If you think you have been in contact with an infected animal then seek medical aid at once.

Tetanus

Travellers should have a booster every five years.

Typhoid

Recommended for all travellers and a booster should be taken every three years.

Always consult your GP when you are travelling abroad, telling him/her all the countries you will be visiting. If you are in any doubt about your vaccination requirements contact:

- Hospital for Tropical Diseases, 4 St Pancras Way, London NW1 0PE. Tel: (071) 387 4411 or (071) 388 8989/9600 (travel clinic) or (0898) 345 081 (pre-recorded healthline).

- Liverpool School of Tropical Medicine, Pembroke Place, Liverpool L3 5QA. Tel: (051) 708 9393 (pre-travel advice and medical queries) or (051) 709 2298 (travel clinic).

- Thomas Cook Vaccination Centre, 45 Berkeley Street, London W1A 1EB. Tel: (071) 499 4000. Vaccinations and certificates provided.

- MASTA (The Medical Advisory Service For Travellers Abroad), London School of Hygiene and Tropical Medicine, Keppel Street, London WC1E 7BR. Tel: (071) 631 4408.

AIDS and HIV

The spread of HIV (human immunodeficiency virus), which leads to AIDS (Acquired Immunodeficiency Syndrome), throughout the world is of particular concern to travellers and everyone working abroad. HIV is contracted through:

- Sexual contact – vaginal, anal or oral sex.
- Blood transfusions with contaminated blood.
- Injections with contaminated needles.

The most likely chance travellers have of contracting HIV is through casual sexual encounters, especially with prostitutes. In many countries you will be approached openly by prostitutes, but this group have a high incidence of HIV — it is claimed that all the prostitutes in Mombasa have HIV and it is thought that a large number of those in Bangkok are infected. Official figures should always be taken with a pinch of salt since some governments, such as that of Thailand, will deny the existence of AIDS in order to protect their revenue from sex-tourism.

The best way to avoid HIV infection is to steer clear of prostitutes and casual sexual encounters: as yet there is no cure and a one-night stand could lead to a terminal illness. If you do have casual sex men should *always* wear a condom and women should insist that their male partners do so. Also, you should have a medical check-up and blood test soon afterwards — if you are infected with HIV you could pass it unknowingly to sexual partners you have in the future.

The chances of becoming infected with HIV through contaminated blood are decreasing due to improved screening processes around the world, but it is still a potentially dangerous situation. However, if you are in the position where you need a blood transfusion it is unlikely you will be in a fit state to make enquiries about the quality of the blood which you are receiving. If you are with other people, one of the group should insist that only blood that has been screened is used. It is also important to know your own blood group — you may be needed to give blood for someone else.

Suggested medical bag

As with other medical matters check with your GP what you should take for particular countries.

- Selection of plasters and bandages (including a continuous roll)
- Elasticated bandages of various sizes
- Paracetamol
- General antibiotic — tetracycline
- Anti-malaria tablets
- Diarrhoea treatment — Imodium
- Rehydration sachets — Dioralyte, Rehydrat
- Anti-AIDS kit — needles, syringes, suturing material
- Condoms
- Travel sickness tablets — Dramamine, Phenergan
- Insect repellent — spray, gel, wipes or roll-on
- Insecticidal spray
- Anti-fungal cream — Canesten
- Antihistamine cream
- Antiseptic cream
- Sun block
- Good quality sunglasses
- Water purification tablets
- Oil of cloves (for toothache)
- Multi-vitamins
- Dusting powder
- Indigestion tablets
- Throat lozenges
- Lip salve
- Cotton wool

All medical items should be packed in a box clearly marked 'First Aid'.

Medical care in Europe

If you are a UK citizen travelling or working in another EU country you are entitled to free, or greatly reduced, medical treatment. To qualify for this you should obtain the DSS leaflet **T2** *Health Advice to Travellers* and complete form **CM1** and send it, at least a month before you are due to leave, to Department of Social Security, Overseas Branch, Newcastle-upon-Tyne NE98 1YX. They will then issue you with an **E111** (E-one-eleven) form which entitles you to medical treatment in any EU country over a twelve month period. You will probably have to pay at the time but if you make sure you get a receipt you will be able to reclaim some, or all, of the medical costs.

Other leaflets worth getting from the DSS are, **SA41** *While You're*

Away and *Your Social Security Health Care and Pension Rights in the European Community.*

PREPARING YOURSELF FOR JOB HUNTING

Since there are an increasing number of people deciding to look for work abroad and it is a competitive market it is a good idea to give yourself every advantage before you go.

What to take with you

If you are hoping to find a job when you arrive in a certain country here are some items that might give you an edge over your rivals:

- Copies of degrees or education certificates. It is a good idea to leave the original documents at home and take a photocopy with you — if it is vital to have the original then you can send for it.

- Letters of introduction or sponsorship. If you know people who have contacts abroad then ask them if they could write you a letter of introduction. This in itself may not get you a job but any contacts abroad are invaluable and this is frequently the first step to finding employment.

- References from previous employers. Take as many references with you as possible — some employers are more impressed with quantity rather than your one glowing reference from Marks and Spencer. If possible get references on headed notepaper as this can have a disproportionately advantageous effect on employers. Do not worry if your references are for a different type of employment to the one you are applying for abroad.

- Take a set of smart clothes. These will not only be needed for interviews but maybe for the jobs themselves. This applies particularly to the hospitality trade and people looking for work in this area should ensure that their smart clothes are hotel and restaurant issue black and whites.

- Take a set of scruffy clothes. Not all interviews are conducted in three-piece suits and not all jobs are done in black and whites. Many temporary jobs are dirty, dusty and smelly. Even if you did not originally intend to work as a manure-shoveller this may be what you end up doing. So take a set of clothes to wear for this eventuality and save your cocktail dress or dinner jacket for evening wear.

- Take a happy disposition — employers respond more positively to cheerful, enthusiastic people.

DO'S AND DON'TS BEFORE YOU GO

Do

- Make sure your passport is up to date and valid for at least three months after your intended date of return.
- Make sure you have adequate insurance — organise it in good time before you leave and ensure that you are covered for the entire period you expect to be overseas.
- Have a contingency plan in case you spend more time overseas than you expected. Ask a relation or friend to extend your insurance if possible — and leave them some money to pay for it.
- Go to your doctor and dentist before you leave. Check on any vaccinations that you need.
- Write to the embassies of the countries you intend to visit. They will be able to tell you the latest situation with regard to visas and work permits.
- Maximise your previous work experience. Have a professional CV (translated if necessary— see Chapter 3), and take as many references as possible.
- Keep possible types of work in mind when you pack your wardrobe.

Don't

- Leave things to the last minute.
- Rely on the 'I'll buy it when I get there' philosophy. Invariably you will suffer from the 'Sorry we've just sold the last one' syndrome.

- Cut any corners as far as health is concerned – being ill abroad can not only cost you a job, it could ultimately lead to you returning home.

- Take it for granted that you will find a job immediately. Be prepared (mentally and monetarily) to spend a few weeks looking for work.

- Give up too easily — finding a temporary job abroad is as much about persistence as it is qualifications and experience.

CHECKLIST

1. Do you have a passport?
   Does it need to be renewed?
   How long will you have to renew it before you leave?

2. Do you have health insurance?
   Does it provide cover for the worst possible scenario?
   Will someone at home have a copy of the policy?

3. Do you know if you will require any work permits or visas?
   Can you get them before you go?
   How long will they take?

4. Do you have enough money?
   Do you have your money in traveller cheques?
   Have you left a copy of their numbers?
   Do you know how to claim a refund if they are lost or stolen?
   Have you a way of paying off your credit cards if you use them?
   Is there a way for money to be sent to you if you lose everything?

5. Have you packed with finding a job in mind?
   Do you have a selection of clothes that could be used for a variety of jobs?

6. Have you got as many references/letters of introduction as possible?
   Will you be carrying them in a safe place?

7. Do you have a contact address in the country you are going to?

3
Achieving High Employability

FINDING SOURCES OF INFORMATION

Just as you would not accept a job in Britain if you knew nothing about what the post would entail, so you should not go looking for work abroad without knowing something about the country in which you hope to work. As well as finding out about the employment situation you should also find out as much general information about the country as possible. This is not just a curiosity-sating exercise — the more you know about a place the quicker you will feel settled and confident, and this is the type of mood you should be in when you begin your job search.

Finding out about foreign countries can be done in a variety of ways:

- Personal experience
- Guidebooks
- Travel books
- Newspapers

Personal experience

Almost everyone knows someone who has been abroad and these contacts should 'have the thumbscrews placed on them' until they tell you everything you want to know. If no one springs immediately to mind for the country in which you hope to work, then ask around — it will be surprising how quickly the grapevine will discover someone who has worked as a shepherd in Tibet.

For specific information about working conditions in a particular country it could be worth putting a small advertisement in a local newspaper. This may provide you with some valuable contacts.

Guidebooks

Guidebooks are a valuable source of information once you get to a country but they should also be read before you leave. They will provide you with a country's history, its customs and also the basic tourist information of where to stay and what to see. For someone with work on their mind addresses of restaurants and hotels can not only be used as places to eat and sleep but also potential places of employment.

Also, look for major festivals and sporting events in a particular country. These invariably attract large numbers of people and where there are people there are employment opportunities.

Some of the major guidebook series are:

- How To Books Limited: Plymbridge House, Estover Road, Plymouth PL6 7PZ. Tel: (0752) 695745. The growing *How To* range covers living and working in a variety of destinations from Australia to Saudi Arabia. Most of the books are geared towards people who want to travel and work.

- Lonely Planet: Lonely Planet Publications, PO Box 617, Hawthorn, Victoria 3122, Australia. Written by travellers for travellers. They produce two series of guides — *On a Shoestring*, which cover several countries, such as South-East Asia or Africa, and *Travel Survival Kits*, which cover individual countries. Over 100 titles cover most areas of the world, although the coverage of European countries is less extensive. The guides are written in a down-to-earth, honest style and pull no punches. Updated every two to three years and one of the best investments for an independent traveller.

- Rough Guides: Harrap Columbus, Chelsea House, 26 Market Square, Bromley, Kent BR1 1NA. Tel: (081) 313 3484. Similar to Lonely Planet in style but with 47 titles their range is not yet as far-reaching. Good coverage of Europe and also parts of Africa, the USA and Central and South America. They give introductory information covering the countries involved and recommendations for the low-priced choices in travel, accommodation and food. Updated every two years, competitively priced and gaining in popularity with travellers.

- Cadogan Guides: Cadogan, 195 Knightsbridge, London SW7 1RE. Tel: (071) 225 2050. Strong coverage of European destinations. Stylishly written and presented, they are aimed at a wide range of travellers, from the independent to the lavish. Worth looking into at the library to see if they will be useful for your purposes.

- Bradt Publications: 41 Nortoft Road, Chalfont St Peter, Bucks SL9 0LA. Tel: (02407) 3478. A valuable *Backpacking Guides* series and now expanding into more general guidebooks for some of the more unusual destinations such as Madagascar and Vietnam. Written by experienced travellers who have been there, done it, and sometimes done it again.

- Let's Go Guides: Harvard Student Agencies Inc, Harvard University, Thayer Hall-B, Cambridge, Mass 02138, USA. Written by Harvard students and updated annually. They cover Europe and America and are designed to show you how to get the most for your money.

- Vacation Work: 9 Park End Street, Oxford OX1 1HJ. Tel: (0865) 241 978. Publishers of the invaluable *Work Your Way Around the World* and other useful titles for employment and study abroad. They are now branching out into *Travel Survival Kits*. Aimed at the budget traveller and written in the same entertaining, practical style as the rest of the Vacation Work titles.

- Travel and Trade Publications: 5 Prince's Buildings, George Street, Bath BA21 2ED. Tel: (0225) 469141. Numerous continental travel guides are published including the *South America Handbook*, the recognised authority on that part of the world.

- Fodor's Guides. Aimed at the more affluent tourist, looking for a bit of luxury. Worth looking at for their practical information, which is of a high standard, and for ideas when you want to splurge a little. Updated annually and more useful than its critics sometimes suggest.

Pocket Guides

The number of publishers producing pocket guidebooks has increased in recent years. The advantages are obvious — size — and they contain a surprising amount of information, particularly if you are planning a short-stay visit. The major series are:

- *American Express pocket guides* — recognised as the best available.
- *Berlitz*
- *Collins Travellers*

- *AA's Essential Guides*
- *Insight Pocket Guides*

By their very nature guidebooks are not 100% accurate and none of them claim to be. The considerable delay between the time of writing and the publication date means that prices will have increased, timetables will have been altered and, in certain cases, the political climate may have changed dramatically.

All these factors should be taken into account when you are reading a guidebook — do not take everything it says as gospel. If you do come across any errors or omissions then you can help the publisher by writing to them and pointing out the changes. They are always delighted to receive this type of information and you may even get a mention in the next edition.

Travel literature

In the last ten years there has been a huge increase in the volume of travel writing being published; the neutral observer could be forgiven for thinking that it is a prerequisite for travellers to produce a book at the end of their wanderings. Few parts of the world have been excluded from this process and it is now possible to experience the world from the comfort of your own living-room.

However, travel literature is not only enjoyable for the armchair traveller, it is also useful for conveying the spirit of a country to people who are planning a visit. You may not pick up too much practical advice from a travel book but you will hear the sounds, smell the smells and feel the sun on your back. There is nothing like a good travel book to inspire a case of wanderlust. Many of these peripatetic writers also work on their travels and so there are some useful tips to be picked up here too.

Whether you read classics of travel literature such as Patrick Leigh Fermor or Wilfred Thesiger, or the modern works of Colin Thubron, Paul Theroux or Jonathan Raban, or the humorous works of Redmond O'Hanlon it is worth dipping into a certain amount of travel literature before you go. It might even give you some ideas for a book of your own.

Newspapers

All the quality daily and Sunday newspapers carry travel sections, which are usually a mixture of first-person accounts and practical advice. These have the great advantage of being reasonably up-to-date and most of them carry valuable Fact Packs about the regions covered. News pages should also be consulted, in order to find out if there has just been a coup in the country you intend to visit or if an earthquake has struck a region you plan to travel through.

WHAT TYPE OF WORK SUITS YOU?

One of the great things about working abroad is that it is an adventure and gives you the chance to do the type of work that you cannot do at home. If you have not thought of doing something totally different then you should — this could be the only chance you have to be a lumberjack in Canada before you return to Britain and work in the same job for the next forty years.

There are some types of work that will not suit everyone, such as demanding physical work, but there are a few questions you should ask yourself before you head off into the wide blue employment yonder:

- Do you enjoy working with people?
- Can you adapt quickly to new situations?
- Will you be able to work in a job where you are required to use a foreign language regularly?
- Do you like physical work, either indoors or outdoors?
- Do you enjoy working with children?
- Are you prepared to turn your hand to something that you would not consider doing at home?

How you answer these questions should determine the type of work you will look for abroad. You may decide you want to work in the hospitality business, or as an au pair, or a labourer, or maybe spend a few weeks on a prawn trawler. Even if you do not have a precise idea of what you want to do, you may have a good idea of what you do not want to do. This will influence your choice of destination — but it is best if you do not close off too many options before you leave.

WHAT TYPE OF WORK IS AVAILABLE?

The ten thousand peseta question. Other than contacts made before you leave (see Chapter 5) the most proven way to find out about what jobs are available in a particular country or region is to sit in a bar for a few hours and get talking to the locals. Although this may result in a bit of a fuzzy head in the morning you may also find that you have made an address-book-full of that invaluable commodity for temporary workers — contacts. You may not have landed a dozen job offers but you could have started a chain of events that will end up with you being in gainful employment.

Another way of discovering what work is available is to check on noticeboards at youth hostels, campsites, shop windows and local centres such as sport centres. People do sometimes advertise for casual workers and it is worth keeping your eyes open for any snippets of information that may lead to some form of employment. Failing this, try placing your own advertisements in prominent places where the locals will see them. Good places to try are local shops and local newspapers.

GETTING EXPERIENCE BEFORE YOU GO

For some jobs abroad it is almost impossible to get experience before you go — not many people can practise being a bullfighter. However, a general rule is 'any experience is good experience'. If you have worked in a variety of jobs and shown that you are adaptable then you will be in a positive and confident frame of mind when you set foot on foreign soil.

In addition to general work experience there are a number of areas that should be considered as providing a valuable asset to the temporary job seeker.

Working in the hospitality industry

All types of jobs in the hospitality industry, from waiting staff to cooks, are in demand abroad. Although experience is not essential it is a good idea to try your hand at this type of work before you go. This will not only provide you with experience which may land you a job but it will give you a chance to see whether you enjoy this working environment.

Working for voluntary organisations

This is an excellent way to get job experience and develop a wide range of skills. To find voluntary work you can either apply through national organisations who specialise in this type of work or offer your services locally — find out where the local care centres are in your area and go and offer your services on a voluntary basis. Or contact local hospitals and see if there is any work you can do there or in the community.

Some organisations who undertake voluntary work in the UK are:

- Community Service Volunteers, 237 Pentonville Road, London N1 9NJ. Tel: (071) 278 6601.
- The Corrymeela Community, Ballycastle, County Antrim BT54 6QU. Tel: (026) 57 62626.
- Edinburgh Cyrenians, 20 Broughton Place, Edinburgh EH1 3RX. Tel: (031) 556 4971.
- Homes for Homeless People, 90–92 Bromham Road, Bedford MK40 2QH. Tel: (0234) 350853.
- Land Use Volunteers, Horticultural Therapy, Goulds Ground, Vallis Way, Frome, Somerset BA11 3DW. Tel: (0373) 464782.
- Leonard Cheshire Foundation, Leonard Cheshire House, 26–29 Maunsel Street, London SW1P 2QN. Tel: (071) 828 1822.
- Reach, 89 Southwark Street, London SE1 0HD. Tel: (071) 928 0452.

Driving

If you do not have a driving licence then it would be a good idea to learn to drive. Although this in itself may not lead to a job it could be a contributory factor with employers. Check to see if you need an international driving licence for the countries you will be visiting. These are required for certain countries and can be obtained from organisations such as the AA.

Teaching English as a foreign language

If you hope to teach English abroad it is possible to get some experience before you go. Summer schools are held around Britain, mostly for foreign school pupils who want to learn English (or whose teachers wants them to learn English) during their summer holidays. These schools take on teachers of English on a temporary basis and it is an excellent way of getting experience of the cut and thrust of teaching English to a group of foreign teenagers.

Further information about summer schools in Britain can be obtained from The British Council, 10 Spring Gardens, London SW1A 2BN.

SELLING YOURSELF BEFORE YOU GO

Writing to prospective employers

If you are applying for jobs before you leave home, the first weapon in your armoury is the initial letter you send advertising your talents. While there may be a great temptation to fill this with pages of prose extolling your personal virtues the golden rules with this type of correspondence are:

- Be brief
- Be precise
- Be clear
- Write in the language of your employer, not your own.

The person who receives your letter will probably be busy and have to deal with dozens of similar missives. They want to be able to see at a glance what your particular qualities are, not read through a tome outlining your life history.

Contents of your letter

Ideally your letter should include:

- Your name and address.

- Your profession — student, teacher, nuclear physicist.

- A brief outline of any relevant qualifications — you can go into greater detail in your accompanying CV.

- What job you are interested in and the length of employment you are seeking.

- A self-addressed envelope for a reply.

- **An International Reply Coupon**. These are available from Post Offices and are used to send return mail from abroad. Check to see how much you will need for the country to which you are writing.

See suggested draft letter in Figure 1.

What not to include

- Waffle — rambling letters will inevitably be filed in the bin.
- Extravagant claims — there is room for bending the truth slightly but lies should be avoided.
- Humour — while a light touch can sometimes reap rewards it is a mistake to try and be funny and crack jokes. For one thing not everyone's sense of humour is the same and once translated into another language your joke may appear obscure at best and obscene at worst.

How to compile a CV

Having caught the employer's attention with your letter of introduction it is then necessary to put some meat on your job-seeking bones. Again this should be done briefly, but at the same time you have to make sure that you have covered all the relevant information.

Most people have a CV of some description. However, this does not mean you should make a few copies of it and send them in an envelope: a CV for purposes in Britain may be different from the one you require for a job abroad. There is nothing wrong with rewriting it for this specific purpose. Some of the main points to consider are:

- Stick to the relevant points — will an overseas employer be interested in the fact that you were a Brownie at the age of ten?
- Emphasise your work experience — detail where you worked and what type of work you did.
- Emphasise any language skills you have — list any languages you can speak and any practical purposes to which you have put them, for instance during an exchange visit to another country.
- List your interests and hobbies, but very briefly.

When you are writing your CV take time to set it out neatly and

Mr Job Hunter
Work Street
Job Town
Great Britain

Mr E. M. Ployer
Market Street
Employmentville
France

[Date]

Dear (Try and find out the exact name of the person)

As a twenty-five-year-old student I am looking for a summer job as a waiter.

I read in Nick Vandome's *How to Find Temporary Work Abroad* of a possible vacancy in your restaurant and I would like to apply for a position.

I have an A level in French and I can speak to a reasonably high conversational level. I also have experience of restaurant work, having worked in both silver service and table service establishments.

I would be available for work from the beginning of July until the end of September.

I enclose my CV and my work references as well as a self-addressed envelope and two International Reply Coupons.

Could you possibly help with this? I look forward to hearing from you at your convenience.

Yours sincerely

Fig. 1. Acceptable letter of application (to be translated if necessary into the language of your prospective employer).

clearly. It should be typed and not handwritten and if you can produce it on a computer then even better. Make sure your printer ribbon is clear and use a reasonably sized typeface — if people have to squint to read what you have written then they may not bother. See the example in Figure 2.

How to get references

If you hope to find a job as a labourer in Australia it will not do you much good if you have a folder full of references singing your praises as a flower arranger. If employers ask for references (and not all of them will, some will take you as they find you) then they will want to see references that are relevant to the job for which you are applying.

The best way to get relevant references is to get in touch with all the previous employers you have worked for (or at least the ones with whom you got on well) and tell them what you are planning to do and ask them if they can provide you with a suitable reference. Make sure that they are aware of the fact that you will be looking for a temporary job abroad rather than a job for life in the City of London and see if they can tailor the reference accordingly.

Almost as important as what is written in the reference is the fact that it is written on official headed notepaper. Prospective employers will be impressed by typed references on official notepaper and it could be the difference between landing a job and being back pounding the streets.

If you cannot find any former employers to give you a reference, or you do not have suitable work experience, ask friends and relations to see if they will produce a reference for you. If you do know someone who will write this type of reference keep it simple and make sure you can live up to its claims.

Compiling an employment 'package'

Writing for a temporary job abroad is about more than running up a brief note about yourself and thrusting it into an overseas-bound envelope. To give yourself a chance you should compile an employment package to send to employers. This should consist of:

- Introductory letter — brief, informative and presented neatly.
- Your work CV — slant it towards your temporary job aspirations and again make sure it is clearly set out.

NAME	Job Hunter
ADDRESS	Work Street Job Town Great Britain
TELEPHONE NUMBER	(071) 333 9999
NATIONALITY	British
DATE OF BIRTH	1/1/1965
QUALIFICATIONS	MA International Relations, St Andrews University
WORK EXPERIENCE	Waiter, Hilton Hotel, London (1989–91) Shop assistant, Marks and Spencer (1991–92) Electrical engineer, Edinburgh (1992–94)
LANGUAGES	French A Level – B Spanish A Level – C Currently studying Italian at night school. In 1986 I spent six weeks in Normandy on a school exchange programme.
INTERESTS	Photography Sailing Breeding snakes
REFERENCES	Enclosed

Fig. 2. Sample CV.

- A photograph of yourself — this never does any harm and can give an employer a better idea of what is being offered. If necessary take a specific photograph for this purpose. A simple head and shoulders shot should suffice and make sure you are looking cheerful rather than dour — a smile is one of the most potent weapons a job seeker can possess.

- References — two or three should be enough for an employer to get an idea of your potential. If possible make sure they are typed (and translated if you are applying to a country where English is not their first language) and on official headed paper.

Present your package in a clear plastic folder and keep all the documents in a logical order, starting with the introductory letter. Do not crush all your documents into a small envelope — if necessary send them in an A4 envelope.

Overcoming language difficulties

The best way to communicate with non-English speakers is to learn their language. In some cases this will be a necessity, in others a courtesy that should be observed, particularly if you are looking for a job. The seriously-minded job seeker may already know at least one foreign language but, if not, it would be a good idea to come to terms with the mother tongues of the countries you will be visiting.

One of the best starting points is local evening classes. These can be located through the invaluable **Training Access Points (TAPs)**, which can be found in most libraries. If you key in a few simple instructions with your requirements TAPs will be able to tell you who offers local courses in the relevant language, where they are and when the courses run. TAPs can also be used if you want to find out information about courses that might be useful when you are abroad, such as hospitality training.

Organisations who offer language courses
These include:

- Accelerated Learning Systems Limited, 50 Aylesbury Road, Aston, Clinton, Aylesbury, Buckinghamshire HP22 5AH. Tel: (0296) 631177. They offer an innovative range of open learning language courses using audio cassettes and suggestopaedia.

- The Berlitz Schools of Language Limited, Wells House, 79

Wells Street, London W1A 3BZ. Tel: (071) 580 6482. They offer language courses with a wide range of teaching materials.

- BBC Enterprises, Woodlands, 80 Wood Lane, London W12 0TT. Courses are offered using videos, audio cassettes and books.

- Centre for Information on Language Teaching and Research, Regent's College, Inner Circle, Regent's Park, London NW1 4NS. Tel: (071) 486 8221.

- Linguaphone, St Giles House, 50 Poland Street, London W1V 4AX. Tel: (071) 734 0574. One of the best known language-learning companies and they not only offer language courses but also support and specific services for the language learner.

Learning a language in this way can be expensive — well over £100 in some cases. But when set against the advantages it will give you when you are looking for a job in a foreign country it is a very worthwhile investment.

Communicating with foreign employers

Imagine you run a business in the UK and you receive a letter written in an unfamiliar language. Out of curiosity you may see if you can get it translated but a much more likely scenario is that you will file it promptly in the wastepaper bin. In the daily hurly-burly of running your business you will have no time to try and decipher a letter which you do not understand. It is exactly the same situation abroad when employers receive letters in a language they do not understand, such as English. They will not even bother to read them and all your careful preparations will have been in vain.

When you are applying for a job abroad even if you speak the language to a reasonable level this does not mean that you will be able to write fluently in that language. In this instance you will need to have your employment package translated. There are a few ways you can go about this:

- Find a native speaker of the language you want translated. Try the well used grapevine of family and friends.

- Approach the language departments of your local university/college/school to see if they can, and will, translate your letter.

If they are willing and able to do this they will probably charge you a fee but this could be negotiable.

- Enlist the services of a translation organisation. These can be found by looking through *Yellow Pages* or you could try one of the following:

  The Institute of Translation and Interpreting, 318a Finchley Road, London NW3 5HT. Tel: (071) 794 9931. They charge between £40 and £65 per 1000 words depending on the language involved and the technical content of the material.

  The Institute of Linguists, 24a Highbury Grove, London N5 2EA. Tel: (071) 359 7445.

TEN STEPS TO FINDING WORK BEFORE YOU GO

1. Choose the countries in which you want to look for a temporary job.

2. Find out as much as you can about these countries — both the countries in general and the employment situation in particular.

3. Choose what type of work you want to do.

4. Get as much relevant experience for this type of work.

5. Compile a relevant, concise and clear employment package.

6. Read Chapter 5 and find as many prospective employers and organisations as possible.

7. Get your employment package translated if necessary.

8. Write to as many employers as possible. Make sure you include a return envelope and a sufficient number of International Reply Coupons. Contacts can be just as important as firm job offers.

9. Learn the language of your target country.

10. Think positively at all times.

4
Areas of Temporary Employment Abroad

JOINING ADVENTURE TRAVEL COMPANIES

An increasingly frequent sight on the overland routes through Africa and Asia are converted Bedford trucks taking travellers on overland tours. These are not only a good way to see the countries involved but the companies also employ drivers, cooks and mechanics. Sometimes the job will involve doing all three in which case you will need either a heavy goods vehicle licence (HGV) or passenger service vehicle licence (PSV). Competition for these places is fierce and many of them are given to experienced drivers and travellers.

Working conditions

- Long hours.
- Mechanical knowledge required.
- Low pay but travel formalities are taken care of.
- Essential to get on with people in claustrophobic conditions.
- Stamina and endurance a must.

Companies to contact

- Dragoman Adventure Travel, Camp Green, Kenton Road, Debenham, Suffolk IP14 6LA. Tel: (0728) 861133.

- Encounter Overland, 267 Old Brompton Road, London SW5 9JA. Tel: (071) 370 6845.

- Exodus Expeditions, 9 Weir Road, Balham, London SW12 0LT. Tel: (081) 675 5550.

- Explore Worldwide Limited, 1 Frederick Street, Aldershot, Hampshire GU11 1LQ.
- Guerba Expeditions, 101 Eden Vale Road, Westbury, Wiltshire BA13 3QX. Tel: (0373) 826611.
- Journey Latin America, 16 Devonshire Road, Chiswick, London W4 2HD. Tel: (081) 747 8315.
- Kumuka Africa, 42 Westbourne Grove, London W2. Tel: (071) 221 2348.
- Top Deck Travel, 131–135 Earls Court Road, London SW5 9RH. Tel: (071) 244 8641.

CAMPING FIRMS

Thousands of people love camping but not everyone enjoys carrying enough equipment for an all-out assault on Everest and then trying to assemble a contraption that would test the skills of Krypton Factor contestants. Several companies realised this a few years ago and this has led to the creation of numerous camping firms who will provide a life under canvas, but without the hassle. These companies choose sites all over Europe and erect fully equipped tents for holidaymakers.

This type of holiday has not only proved to be extremely popular but it is also a godsend for people who want to work overseas — thousands of workers are taken on every year, either as on-site couriers or the muscle to put up and take down the tents.

Companies to contact

- Canvas Holidays, 12 Abbey Park Road, Dunfermline, Fife KY12 7PD. Tel: (0383) 621000. Operate in Austria, France, Germany, Italy, Spain and Switzerland.
- Eurocamp Travel Ltd, Edmundson House, Tatton Street, Knutsford, Cheshire WA16 6BG. Tel: (0565) 650022. Austria. Belgium, France, Germany, Italy, Netherlands, Spain and Switzerland.
- Club 18–30, Academic House, 24–28 Oval Road, London NW1 7DE. Tel: (071) 485 4141. France, Greece, Spain and Turkey.

- Eurosites, Wavell House, Holcombe Road, Helmshore, Lancashire BB4 4NB. Tel: (0706) 228687. Austria, Belgium, France, Germany, Italy, Luxembourg and Spain.

- Drive Europe, 40 Market Place South, Leicester LE1 5HB. Tel: (0533) 620644. France, Italy and Spain.

- Club Cantabrica Holidays Ltd, 146/148 London Road, St. Albans, Herts AL1 1PQ. Tel: (0727) 33141. France, Greece, Italy and Spain.

- ILG Coach and Camping, Devonshire House, 29–31 Elmfield Road, Bromley, Kent BR1 1LT. Tel: (081) 466 6660. France and Spain.

- Quest Travel, Oliver House, 18 Marine Parade, Brighton, Sussex BN2 1TL. Tel: (0273) 677777. Austria, France, Germany and Italy.

- Seasun/Tentrek, 4 East Street, Colchester, Essex CO1 2XW. Tel: (0206) 861886. France, Italy, Spain and Portugal.

- Solaire Holidays, 1158 Stratford Road, Hall Green, Birmingham B28 8AF. Tel: (021) 778 5061. France and Spain.

Types of jobs available

Couriers

Each company has at least one courier at each of its sites. Their job is to welcome the new arrivals, make sure their tent is clean and tidy and answer any queries they have. This may sound simple but the couriers usually end up being a cross between childminder, games organiser, tourist information officer, social organiser and crisis manager. Needless to say there is never a dull moment.

Couriers need to have a knowledge of the language of the country in which they hope to work because they will have to liaise with the campsite owners and the locals.

Companies generally employ students but they are now branching out and employing a greater number of older people, including retired couples. The jobs last for approximately three months during the summer and the wages can be anything from £200 to £450 a month, with free accommodation. Most posts are filled by January but there is a high drop-out rate so if you are on a waiting list it may be worthwhile getting in touch with the company at regular intervals.

Flying squad member/driver

A more mobile job than couriers as these are the people who travel around to all the campsites and put up and dismantle the tents. This usually takes place during March/April and September although some of the Flying Squad members and drivers are kept on for the whole summer as troubleshooters. No knowledge of a foreign language is required but the applicants should be fit, enthusiastic and possess a good sense of humour. Drivers usually need to be over twenty-three years old for insurance purposes.

SKI RESORT COMPANIES

For snow-lovers the prospect of a job in a ski resort is an appealing one. There are a number of companies who employ a variety of staff over the winter season and people who are interested should get their applications in as early as May.

For people interested in working as ski instructors it could be worth contacting The British Association of Ski Instructors (BASI) Inverdruie Visitors Centre, Aviemore, Inverness-shire PH22 1RL. Tel: (0479) 810407.

Companies to contact

- Activity Travel, 23 Blair Street, Edinburgh EH1 1QZ. Tel: (031) 225 9457.
- Balkan Holidays, 19 Conduit Street, London W1R 9TD. Tel: (071) 491 4499.
- Inghams, 10–18 Putney Hill, London SW15 6AX. Tel: (081) 89 6555.
- Kuoni Travel, Kuoni House, Dorking, Surrey RH5 4AZ. Tel: (0396) 744444.
- Neilson, 71 Hough Side Road, Pudsey, Leeds LS28 9BR. Tel: (0532) 393020.

- Panorama Ski Experience, 29 Queens Road, Brighton BN1 3YN. Tel: (0273) 206531.

- Poles Apart, 119 Hampstead Way, London NW11 7JN. Tel: (081) 455 2214.

- Simply Ski, 8 Chiswick Terrace, Acton Lane, London W4 5LY. Tel: (081) 742 2541.

- Ski Val, 41 North End Road, London W14 8SZ. Tel: (071) 371 4900.

- Ski West, 1 Belmont, Lansdowne Road, Bath BA1 5DZ. Tel: (0225) 444516.

- Thomson, Greater London House, Hampstead Road, London NW1. Tel: (071) 387 9321.

Pay and working conditions (per week)

- Resort managers — £70–£90.
- Cooks — £60–£80.
- Chalet staff — £40.
- Ski guides — £50–£75.

Most resort workers are expected to work long hours for moderate wages. However, food and accommodation are usually provided and there are ample opportunities for skiing.

TEACHING ENGLISH AS A FOREIGN LANGUAGE (TEFL)

In recent years teaching English as a foreign language has become something of a boom industry. Not so much because people around the world have recently discovered a burning desire to learn English (although this is definitely a contributory factor), but because there has been a vast increase in the number of TEFL-qualified globetrotters.

There are two ways to go about teaching English as a foreign language: take a recognised TEFL course, or go somewhere where they want to learn English and rely on your natural charm and ability. Both ways have been proven to work.

Many TEFL jobs are for a longer duration than the temporary

worker is willing to spend but there are an equal number for a few weeks or months. TEFL is one way of finding work in those notoriously difficult locations for temporary workers — Africa, Asia and South America. From Zimbabwe to Taiwan people are eager to learn English and most of them are only concerned that you can speak the language yourself. If you want to work in one of these countries then you should seriously consider TEFL.

Obtaining recognised qualifications

In recent years there has been a marked increase in the number of organisations offering TEFL qualifications. These vary greatly in intensity, quality and price. The standard recognised qualification is the Royal Society of Arts (RSA)/University of Cambridge Local Examinations Syndicate (UCLES) Certificate for Teaching English as a Foreign Language to Adults. This is an intensive, practical course (four weeks if you undertake it on a full-time basis) and competition for places is stiff. You will have to attend an interview, at which you may be given a short written test dealing with common grammatical and semantic problems that may occur while you are teaching. With this in mind it would be a good idea to take a look at either *Rediscover Grammar* by D Crystal (Longman) or *Discover English* by R Bolitho and B Tomlinson (Heinemann).

How much will it cost?

Most RSA Certificate courses cost in the region of £700–£800. Although this is a large lump sum to pay out it is worth remembering that the Certificate is highly thought of around the world and once you have it you will be able to virtually pick a job in the country of your choosing. Look at it as a valuable investment.

Where can you do the course?

RSA Certificate courses are held at centres all over Britain. Three of the main ones are:

- International House, 106 Piccadilly, London W1V 9FL. Tel: (071) 491 2598.

- International Languages Centres Limited, White Rock, Hastings, East Sussex TN34 1JY. Sister centre of International House and they have a computerised database which matches applicants with TEFL qualifications to jobs primarily in the Middle or Far East.

- Bell School of Languages, 1 Redcross Lane, Cambridge CB2 2QX. They run courses in Cambridge, Norwich, Saffron Walden, Bath and London.

For a list of other centres offering RSA Certificates contact:

- UCLES, 1 Hills Road, Cambridge CB1 2EU.
- RSA, 8 John Adam Street, London WC2N 8EY.
- British Council, English Language Information Unit, 10 Spring Gardens, London SW1A 2BN.

Other available qualifications

In addition to the RSA Certificate there are numerous other introductory TEFL courses around the country. Some of these have the advantage of being taught by organisations who have language schools abroad, so once you have gained your qualification you are very likely to be given a job with them.

Contact the following:

- Trinity College, 11–13 Mandeville Place, London W1Y 6AQ. Offer courses in Teaching English to Speakers of Other Languages (TESOL) at their centres around the country. As intensive as the RSA Certificate but slightly cheaper. A well thought of alternative which allows you to teach children too.

- Inlingua Method Courses, Essex House, Temple Street, Birmingham B2 5DB. Tel: (021) 643 3472. Ten day courses. Designed specifically for their schools abroad. Also run courses in Barcelona, Madrid, Lisbon, Rome, Cairo and Rio.

- Linguarama, New Oxford House, 16 Waterloo Street, Birmingham B2 5UG. Tel: (021) 632 5925. Courses in Birmingham, Manchester, Nottingham, Winchester and Canterbury. Five-and-a-half days in duration.

- Primary House, 300 Gloucester Road, Horfield, Bristol BS7 8PD. Tel: (0272) 311119. Jobs in Greece virtually guaranteed for those who pass the weekend course and then a home-study course.

- Stenson Learning Centre, 25 Eggesford Road, Stenson Fields, Derby DE24 3BH. Run a TEFL correspondence diploma course.

- Surrey Language Centre, Sandford House, 39 West Street, Farnham, Surrey GU9 7DR. Tel: (0262) 723494. One week courses.

How to get a job

English as a Foreign Language (EFL) positions around the world are advertised in several publications including, the *Times Educational Supplement*, the *Education Guardian* (Tuesdays) and the *EFL Gazette* (Loop Format Limited, 10 Wright's Lane, London W8 6TA).

If you have an RSA Certificate and some TEFL experience (remember, there are numerous language schools in Britain at which you can teach before you go abroad) then you could apply to the British Council for a teaching job overseas. They are the largest international EFL employer and have 52 teaching centres around the world. Even with the above qualifications they may require a TEFL RSA Diploma, which can be undertaken after the Certificate, and two years' teaching experience. For further information contact Central Management of Direct Teaching, 10 Spring Gardens, London SW1A 2BN.

Other organisations who employ people with RSA Certificates and teaching experience include:

- Bell Educational Trust, Overseas Department, The Lodge, Redcross Lane, Cambridge CB2 2QX.

- ILC Recruitment, 1 Riding House, London W1A 3AS.

- English Worldwide, 17 New Concordia Wharf, Mill Street, London SE1 2BB. Advertised as 'the complete EFL recruitment service'.

- International House, (as above), recruit for their 85 affiliated schools worldwide.

In some language schools abroad you will be asked to work long hours for only moderate wages. You may be given accommodation and you can supplement your salary with private teaching. If you put up a notice in the school or college you will invariably find a number of students who want additional tuition.

It is possible to find TEFL work without any previous experience or qualifications. You will need to be bolder and pushier but if you are confident in your own ability then this is often enough to convince other people.

VOLUNTARY ORGANISATIONS

A temporary job abroad does not have to earn you large sums of money for it to be beneficial and worthwhile. Voluntary work, by its very nature, may not be as well paid as some other forms of employment but it has a number of advantages of its own:

- Very satisfying form of work.
- Wide variety of types of voluntary work.
- The chance of working in countries that might otherwise be unavailable to the temporary worker.
- Voluntary work abroad always looks good on a CV.

Despite signs to the contrary voluntary organisations usually do pay their staff. However, these are generally very small amounts that are pocket money more than anything else. It is also worth remembering that many voluntary organisations require the participants to pay a significant amount of the cost involved in getting them to the area in which they are going to work. But for people who want to try something totally different, and are not afraid to work hard in sometimes trying circumstances, voluntary work should be looked at as a serious option.

Action Health 2000

Contact: 25, Gwydir Street, Cambridge CB1 2LG. Tel: (0223) 460853.
Dedicated to establishing better health care in Africa and Asia.
Age: 21+.
Countries: India, Tanzania, Zambia, Zimbabwe.
Duration: 6 months–2 years.
Type of work: Opportunities for doctors, nurses, midwives, health visitors, physiotherapists and speech therapists.
Finances: Volunteers are required to provide approximately £750 towards the cost of the entire project but this can vary considerably. Volunteers receive accommodation, food, insurance, travel costs and pocket money.

Qualifications: Appropriate medical qualifications and experience.

Agency for Personal Service Overseas

Contact: 30 Fitzwilliam Square, Dublin 2, Ireland. Tel: 01 614411.

Promote and sponsor development in third world countries.

Age: 21+.

Countries: Over 40 developing countries. The majority of them are in Africa.

Duration: Usually two years.

Type of work: Administration, agriculture, education, engineering/construction, medicine and social sciences.

Finances: Return air fare, insurance, accommodation and a living allowance are provided.

Qualifications: Volunteers must be Irish nationals. Basic skills or qualifications are required but experience is not essential.

ATD Fourth World

Contact: 48 Addington Square, London SE5 7LB.

An international human rights organisation involved with helping some of the most disadvantaged people around the world.

Age: 18+.

Countries: Belgium, Burkina Faso, Canada, Central African Republic, Germany, Guatemala, Haiti, Honduras, Ivory Coast, Luxembourg, Madagascar, Mauritius, Netherlands, Philippines, Réunion, Senegal, Spain, Sri Lanka, Switzerland, Thailand and United States.

Type of work: Working in disadvantaged communities, helping people build a better future for themselves.

Duration: Initially three months. Volunteers who want to stay on after this can apply for one or two year placements.

Finances: For the first month volunteers are required to pay for their own food. For the next two months accommodation and food are provided. Insurance is also provided.

Qualifications: No specific professional or academic qualifications are required.

British Executive Service Overseas

Contact: 164 Vauxhall Bridge Road, London SW1V 2RB. Tel: (071) 630 0644.

Business people are recruited to give advice to developing countries in the fields of industry and commerce, science, trade and commerce, and industry.

Age: Volunteers should be retired business people, or executives on secondment from their employers.

Countries: Fifty countries in the developing world, eastern and central Europe.

Type of work: All areas of business advice.

Duration: Usually 2–3 months. Maximum of six months.

Finances: Travel, accommodation, food, insurance and expenses are paid to volunteers.

Qualifications: Volunteers should have a solid business record and an ability to pass on their knowledge to businesses in developing countries.

Centro Studi Terzo Mondo

Contact: Via G B Morgagni 29, 20129 Milan, Italy. Tel: 010 02 2940 9041.

An organisation for people of all nationalities that has a wide-ranging commitment to developing projects in the Third World.

Age: 18+.

Countries: Angola, Brazil, Chad, Ecuador, Ethiopia, India, Indonesia, Mozambique, Peru and Somalia.

Duration: Open ended.

Type of work: Projects are undertaken which require teachers, medical staff, social workers and community workers.

Finances: Accommodation and food are provided. Volunteers also receive $100 per week pocket money and insurance.

Qualifications: They are preferred for specific postings but they are not always essential.

Christian Outreach

Contact: 1 New Street, Leamington Spa, Warwickshire CV31 1HP. Tel: (0926) 3153301.

Age: 22+.

Countries: Cambodia, Sudan and Thailand.

Duration: One year.

Type of work: A wide range of volunteers are required including nurses, midwives, nutritionists, engineers, sanitation experts, builders, electricians, mechanics and community development workers.

Finances: Accommodation and food, plus £50 per week pocket money.

Qualifications: Applicants should have qualifications in the relevant fields, and a Christian commitment.

Concordia (Youth Service Volunteers)

Contact: 8 Brunswick Place, Hove, East Sussex BN3 1ET. Tel: (0273) 772086.

Works in conjunction with European voluntary youth organisations which organise international work camps.

Age: 17–30.

Countries: France, Germany, Latvia, Tunisia and Turkey.

Duration: Most of the camps last for 2–3 weeks between the end of June and mid-September. A few camps are available during Easter, usually in France or Germany.

Type of work: Varied — conservation, construction, social work and some teaching of English.

Finances: Volunteers are required to pay an application fee and also their own travel costs. Food and accommodation are provided free of charge at the work camps.

The Cranfield Trust

Contact: 6c Frognal Mansions, 97 Frognal, London NW3 6XT. Tel: (071) 794 6487.

Maintains a database of volunteers who can help charities by sharing their technical expertise. Volunteers act as advisers and people with skills in engineering, disaster appraisal and languages are required to join the International Rescue Corps to help in times of disaster.

East European Partnership

Contact: 15 Princeton Court, 53–55 Felsham Road, London SW15 1AZ. Tel: (081) 780 2841.

Volunteers are placed in full-time jobs in various Eastern European countries.

Age: In general 20–70.

Countries: Bulgaria, Czech and Slovak Republics, Hungary, Poland and Romania.

Type of work: Teaching (mostly of English) and child care (Romania).

Duration: Minimum of two years for teachers and one year for child care workers.

Finances: Volunteers are paid a salary at local rates and are also provided with return travel, pre-departure grant and re-equipment grant on return home.

Qualifications: Teaching qualifications and experience for teaching posts and NNEB and CQSW for child care in Romania.

Frontiers Foundation/Operation Beaver

Contact: 2615 Danforth Avenue, Suite 203, Toronto, M4C 1L6, Canada. Tel: (416) 690 3930.

Helps local communities with basic housing needs and reducing poverty.

Age: 18+.

Country: Canada (Alberta, Ontario and Northwest Territories).

Duration: 12 weeks and over, usually during June–August.

Type of work: Physically demanding manual work as volunteers are required to help build and renovate log houses.

Finances: Volunteers have to pay for their own fare to Canada. Once there they are provided with accommodation, food, local travel expenses and insurance. A moderate living allowance is provided after the first 12 weeks.

Qualifications: No specific qualifications are required but volunteers must be physically fit.

Girl Guides Association (UK)

Contact: 17–19 Buckingham Palace Road, London SW1W 0PT. Tel: (071) 834 6242.

Age: 18+.

Countries: India, Mexico and Switzerland.

Duration: Varies.

Type of work: Assisting the development of Guide Associations, training adult leaders and administrative duties at overseas centres.

Finances: Volunteers usually have to pay their own travel costs to their destination. Thereafter accommodation, food and pocket money are provided.

Qualifications: Volunteers must be members of the Girl Guide Association.

International Cooperation for Development (ICD)

Contact: Unit 3, Canonbury Yard, 190a New North Road, London N1 7BJ. Tel: (071) 354 0883.

Recruits professionally qualified and experienced people for projects in the Third World to tackle poverty and promote development.

Age: No specific restrictions.

Countries: Dominican Republic, Ecuador, El Salvador, Honduras, Namibia, Nicaragua, Peru, Yemen, Zimbabwe.

Type of work: Health care, agriculture, education, environment and public health, cooperative/small business training, computer and information technology.

Duration: Minimum two years.

Finances: Workers are paid a salary based on local rates. In addition, there is also a UK allowance, return flights, pre-departure grant and insurance.

Qualifications: Applicants should have a qualification in their relevant field of experience and also two years' work experience.

International Health Exchange

Contact: Africa Centre, 38 King Street, London WC2E 8JT. Tel: (071) 836 5833.

A coordinating agency for experienced health workers.

Age: 18+.

Countries: Worldwide, with particular emphasis in Africa, Asia, the Caribbean, Latin America and the Pacific.

Duration: Usually 1–2 years but there are some opportunities for placements of a few months.

Type of work: Doctors, nurses, physiotherapists, nutritionists, health administrators and health educators.

Finances: Vary according to the country in which the volunteer is working.

Qualifications: All volunteers should have the relevant qualifications and experience in their own field.

Joint Assistance Centre

Contact: H-65, South Extension 1, New Delhi 11049, India.

A group dedicated to disaster assistance in India. They work in cooperation with other voluntary agencies.

Age: 18+.

Country: India.

Duration: 3–6 months.

Type of work: General disaster assistance including organising playschemes, organising fundraising, teaching English and increasing awareness.

Finances: Volunteers must make their own way to India and are then required to contribute approximately £60 per month towards the cost of the operation. Accommodation is provided but volunteers must pay for their own food.

Qualifications: Experience is considered useful but not essential.

Latin Link

Contact: Whitefield House, 186 Kennington Park Road, London SE11 4B. Tel: (071) 582 4952.

Short-term projects in Latin America designed to demonstrate the interdependence of the worldwide church.

Age: 18–35.

Countries: Argentina, Bolivia, Brazil, Nicaragua and Peru.

Duration: Two teams — spring for 4 months, summer for 7 weeks.

Type of work: Wide ranging — from evangelism to bricklaying and carpentry.

Finances: Volunteers are required to pay for all travel and living expenses. This is approximately £1500.

Qualifications: Volunteers must have a Christian commitment.

The Mission To Seamen's Voluntary Service Scheme

Contact: St Michael Paternoster Royal, College Hill, London EC4R 2RL. Tel: (071) 248 5202/7442.

Opportunities for Christian service in the seafaring world.

Age: 18–24.

Countries: In ports worldwide.

Duration: One year.

Type of work: Christian ministry within the shipping industry.

Qualifications: Must be an Anglican, or a member of another Christian denomination prepared to participate fully in Anglican ministry and worship. A clean driving licence is required.

Richmond Fellowship International

Contact: The Coach House, 8 Addison Road, London W14 8DL. Tel: (071) 603 2442.

The largest international voluntary organisation involved with community mental health.

Age: 22+.

Countries: United States and some eastern European and developing countries.

Duration: One year.

Type of work: Social therapy including gardening, cooking, art, music, drama and sport. Volunteers can also work as administrative and financial advisers.

Finances: Accommodation and food are provided, plus an allowance of approximately £27 per week.

Qualifications: Experienced volunteers with professional training in nursing, social work or psychology.

Scottish Churches World Exchange

Contact: 6A Randolph Place, Edinburgh EH3 7TE. Tel: (031) 225 8115.

Places volunteers with an aim for them to become part of the local church and community.

Age: 18+.

Countries: Africa, Asia, Central America, Europe and the Middle East.

Duration: 6–18 months.

Type of work: Varies according to volunteers' interests and skills.

Finances: Although accommodation, food and pocket money are provided volunteers are expected to raise at least £1500 towards the cost of the project.

Qualifications: Volunteers must be members of Scottish churches or live in Scotland and show a commitment to working in the church abroad.

Skillshare Africa

Contact: Recruitment/Selection, Skillshare Africa, 3 Belvoir Street, Leicester LE1 6Sl. Tel: (0523) 541862.

Qualified and experienced workers are required for work in four southern African countries.

Age: No specific restrictions.

Countries: Botswana, Lesotho, Mozambique and Swaziland.

Type of work: Most professional fields including health, education, engineering and community development.

Duration: Two years.

Finances: Accommodation, a living allowance, return flight and grants for equipment are provided.

Qualifications: Professional qualifications and a minimum of two years' post-qualification experience.

United Nations Association (Wales) International Youth Service

Contact: Welsh Centre for International Affairs, Cathays Park, Cardiff CF1 3AP. Tel: (0222) 223088.

Volunteers work on short-term voluntary projects overseas.

Age: 17–18+.

Countries: Africa, eastern and western Europe, India, North America and Russia.

Type of work: Archaeology, conservation, construction, cultural schemes, playschemes, reconstruction, renovation and special needs projects.

Duration: Up to four weeks.

Finances: Volunteers pay a nominal registration fee and their own travelling expenses. Accommodation and food are provided free of charge for the duration of the project.

Qualifications: Previous experience is required for people wishing to work on projects in developing countries.

Voluntary Service Overseas (VSO)

Contact: 9 Belgrave Square, London SW1X 8PW. Tel: (081) 780 1331.

Volunteers are placed in full-time jobs in developing countries.

Age: Usually 21–70.

Countries: Africa, Asia, the Caribbean and the Pacific.

Type of work: Agriculture, communications, health, legal, librarianship, medical, social and business development, and technical.

Duration: Minimum of two years.

Finances: A maintenance allowance is paid based on local salary levels. Return flight, accommodation and a clothing allowance are also provided.

Qualifications: Technical skills, professional qualifications and relevant work experience.

Winant Clayton Volunteer Association

Contact: 38 Newark Street, London E1 2AA. Tel: (071) 375 0547.

This is a community service volunteer scheme based in the USA.

Age: Minimum of 18 but over 19 is preferred.

Country: USA.

Type of work: Working with various care agencies who deal with issues such as children, homelessness, AIDS, the elderly and psychiatric rehabilitation.

Duration: Three months from mid-June to mid-September. (This includes one free month for independent travel). Application forms should be returned by 15 January each year.

Finances: Volunteers are required to pay their own fares and insurance. Accommodation, food and pocket money are provided while working but volunteers should have enough extra money for their month of travel.

WorldTeach

Contact: Harvard Institute for International Development, 1 Eliot Street, Cambridge, Massachusetts 02138-5705, USA. Tel: 617

495 5527. An organisation devoted to contributing to education overseas and providing opportunities for people to gain experience in international development.

Age: 18+.

Countries: China, Costa Rica, Ecuador, Poland, Russia, South Africa and Thailand.

Duration: One year.

Type of work: The majority of the work is teaching English but there are some openings for teaching science, mathematics and sport. Volunteers can work in primary or secondary schools, colleges, universities and non-profit-making organisations.

Finances: Volunteers are required to pay for the cost of the programme. This is approximately $3,400, which covers air fares, insurance and support for the year.

Qualifications: Anyone can apply but applicants must be fluent in English and show a commitment to teaching abroad.

WORK CAMPS

Work camps are run by voluntary organisations and they generally operate for 2–4 weeks. Their aim is to bring together people of different cultures and races to work on a specific project within the community. The type of project varies greatly from country to country but the overall goal is to enhance local initiatives rather than replace them. Work camps are not undertaken if the work can be done by local labour. The type of work undertaken covers ecology, Third World solidarity, children, peace, disability, anti-racism and renovation. There are leaders at all work camps and these are volunteers, usually in their early 20s.

There are several organisations worldwide who run work camps. In Britain the biggest work camp organisation is:

International Voluntary Service (IVS)

Contact: Old Hall, East Bergholt, near Colchester CO7 6TQ. Tel: (0206) 298215. (South); 188 Roundhay Road, Leeds LS8 5PL. Tel: (0532) 406787 (North); or St John's Church Centre, Princes Street, Edinburgh EH2 4BJ. Tel: (031) 229 7318.

Countries: Albania, Algeria, Australia, Austria, Baltic States, Belgium, Bulgaria, CIS, Czech Republic, Denmark, Finland, France, Germany, Greece, Hungary, Italy, Morocco, Netherlands, Norway, Poland, Portugal, Romania, Slovenia, Spain, Sweden, Switzerland, Tunisia, Turkey, USA. IVS also operate work camps in the UK.

Age: 18+.

Conditions of service: Accommodation is provided, usually in a village hall or a community centre. Volunteers work for 30–40 hours a week but evenings and weekends are usually free. Volunteers should be fit enough to undertake the work at their particular camp and in some cases they may have to face additional emotional strain.

Finances: Volunteers must pay a registration fee when they apply to join a work camp. Registration for up to two camps in 1993 is:

Europe: Waged £75, Student £65, Unwaged £60.

Eastern Europe: Waged £85, Student £75, Unwaged £70.

In addition to this volunteers must also provide their own travel costs to and from the camps. In return accommodation and food is provided free of charge at the camps.

Type of work: There is no typical work camp and volunteers could find themselves working on a boat in the Baltic or in a mountain village in Switzerland.

Other organisations

Other organisations which run work camps are:

- Christian Movement for Peace (CMP), Bethnal Green United Reform Church, Pott Street, London E2 2OF. Tel: (071) 729 7985.
- Concordia (Youth Service Volunteers) (see above).
- Quaker International Social Projects (QISP), Friends House, Euston Road, London NW1 2BJ. Tel: (071) 387 3601.
- United Nations Association (UNA), International Youth Service, Temple of Peace, Cathays Park, Cardiff CF1 3AP.

These organisations operate all over the world and work camps are an excellent opportunity to work in areas of the world which might otherwise be closed to the temporary worker.

WORKING FOR YOUTH ORGANISATIONS

BUNAC

Contact:

The British Universities North America Club (BUNAC)
16 Bowling Green Lane
London EC1R 0BD.
Tel: (071) 251 0215.

or

c/o Union of Students in Ireland (USIT)
19 Aston Quay
Dublin 2.
Tel: 778117.

Since the early 1960s BUNAC has been known as an excellent outlet for employment in North America, which is notoriously difficult to penetrate. While this aspect of BUNAC is going from strength to strength they have added Australia, Jamaica and Malta to their repertoire. They also have a number of other strings to their bow.

Bunacamp

A well established and popular programme which sends camp counsellors to children's summer camps in America and Canada. They offer formal instruction in sports, arts and crafts, drama, nature, computers and science. Anyone between 19½ and 35 is eligible to apply (students and non-students), but you must enjoy working with children and preferably have held a leadership role such as school prefect, youth leader, scout or guide. A qualification in sports, crafts or music may help you obtain a position as a specialist counsellor but this is by no means essential. The most important qualification is a positive personality and a keen participation in a relevant hobby or interest.

There are three types of camps: agency camps, which are general camps with scouts, guides and inner city children; specialist camps for handicapped children; specialist camps teaching one sport, such as tennis. The counsellors work for approximately two months and they are then free to travel around America.

Interviews take place during the first and second terms of the university year and interested parties should get their applications in as soon as possible, as interviews are arranged on a first-come-first-served basis. Having said that, *all* first-time applicants are interviewed.

Successful applicants will have to pay a £55 (1993 figures) registration fee (62 punts in Ireland) and join BUNAC for £3.50. For this BUNAC will provide you with:

- Return air fare.
- J-1 Work and Travel Visa.
- Travel to and from your camp.

- Your food and lodgings for the period you are at the camp.
- A salary of $390 or $450. This is in total for your time at camp and includes deductions for your air fare and the suchlike.

KAMP (Kitchen and Maintenance Programme)

This is ideal for people who would like to work on a summer camp but do not want to work directly with children. It is similar to Bunacamp in that air fares and visas are arranged in advance but it differs in that you can choose what type of work you want to do (BUNAC has a directory of the various jobs). The choices available include working in the kitchen, dining room, cooking (some experience needed), maintenance, being a porter, cleaning and driving.

Applicants must be members of BUNAC, be in full-time tertiary education studying a degree course or an HND and be available for work by June. The registration fee is £64 and during the time you are on KAMP you will receive a total minimum salary of $520. You will be able to travel in America for approximately six weeks after you leave.

Work America

One of the best ways to work in America and one of the very few that will allow you to legally do casual work in this country.

Any current, full-time student doing a tertiary or postgraduate course at degree or HND level in England, Scotland or Wales (students in Northern Ireland should apply through USIT) is eligible. The programme provides students with a place on the 'Exchange Visitor Program' and the invaluable J-1 visa with which you can then travel and work in any part of America. You can either arrange a job before you go — BUNAC will aid you in this with their free Job Directory — or you can be sponsored by an American citizen. If you know someone in America who would be prepared to do this it is the ideal situation because you can then go your own way and find work as you go.

The registration fee for Work America is £80 and on top of this you will need the cost of your flight (approximately £379) and insurance (£85 or £105), both of which BUNAC will help organise for you, and proof of personal funds of between $300 and $600. Although this may seem like a large outlay compared with BUNACAMP or KAMP remember that you will be working in a job with a realistic salary — the average weekly income on the programme is £150. All successful applicants are required to attend an orientation course in December.

Work Canada

Similar to Work America but with two important differences:

1. You have to be returning to full-time tertiary education, which precludes final-year students but allows people who are taking a year off between school and university, providing they have an unconditional place at a university, polytechnic or college.

2. The scheme lasts for up to six months.

An ideal way to work for a short period in a country with plenty of temporary job opportunities. The registration fee is £72 and you need proof of funds of between $500 and $1000.

Work Australia

Open to any UK citizen between 17 and 26. Similar to making your own way on a Holiday Working Visa but BUNAC offer help with booking flights and arranging insurance and an information service with their co-operators, the Student Service Australia (SSA). Advice can be sought from them throughout your time Down Under.

Work Jamaica

A relatively new and small programme which provides full-time students in Britain with the opportunity of working in Jamaica during the summer. Although it is a self-help programme, like Work America and Work Canada, it is not a self-financing operation and monetary gain is not its aim. People who have been on the programme relate that the experience gained is far greater than the contents of a pay packet.

The programme, which costs between £750–£800, depending on whether you go in June or July, includes flight, accommodation on arrival, orientation, work permission and insurance. There is also back-up support from the Jamaica Organisation of Youth & Student Tourists (JOYST).

Work Malta

This is a new scheme, available to catering students only, which provides opportunities for work in resort areas. The programme will be in the second year of operation in 1993.

Camp America
Contact:

American Institute of Foreign Study (UK) Ltd
37A Queens Gate
London SW7 5HR.
Tel: (071) 589 3223.

Similar in many respects to BUNACAMP. The main options offered are:

Camp Counsellor. Specialist or general. Pocket-money wages range from $140-$350, depending on age. Counsellors can earn an additional $150 if they have lifesaving skills.

Campower. As with KAMP and only available to students. Wages are $350 for the nine-week period of the camp.

Family companion. This is a programme which places the applicant with American families and he or she has responsibilities for helping to look after the host family's children. Applicants must be 18–24, possess a full driving licence and preferably be non-smokers.

Au pair
A further option is also offered: the chance to spend a year in America on the Au Pair in America programme. If you are aged 18–25 you can get more information about this programme from:
Au Pair in America, Dept. CA, 37 Queens Gate, London SW7 5HR. Tel: (071) 581 2730.

Camp counsellors are also employed by:
Camp Counsellors USA, 154A Heath Road, Twickenham, Middlesex TW1 4BN.

5
The World at a Glance

This section covers the countries where temporary work is most readily available. Most of the information is for people who want to organise a job before they leave the UK. However, being in the right place at the right time is sometimes more important than having all the right papers and qualifications, and packing your bags on a whim can, in some cases, be the best course of action.

Each listing includes a few addresses of prospective employers. These are not exhaustive by any means and they will only be able to provide jobs for a small number of people. In some cases the addresses may only be useful in order to locate the establishment once you arrive in the country. However, when writing to employers it would be worth asking if they could provide you with some more addresses of people offering a similar kind of work — although one restaurateur may not have any vacancies he may have contacts who are looking for some temporary workers. As with most things concerned with temporary jobs abroad you have to be bold and not afraid to ask.

Many of the organisations listed below operate by giving you a job before you go abroad. If this is the case you should make sure that you get the job offer in writing stating:

- The duration of employment.
- The type of work you will be doing.
- The rate of pay.
- Whether you will have to pay your fare to your destination.
- Whether you will be provided with insurance.

- Whether you will be provided with accommodation and, if so, whether you will have to pay for it or not.

If you do not receive written confirmation of a job, or you have any doubts about it, then you should not commit yourself. While most organisations that deal with working abroad are highly reputable there are always operators who are willing to take advantage of working travellers.

Officially organised temporary work is not the only way to work abroad — as many people adopt a freelance approach as those who go through the official channels. Some countries have strict regulations aimed at deterring freelance job seekers so, in order to avoid any difficulty, the opportunities listed below deal with official organisations and with countries who welcome people adopting the freelance method.

One publication that is worth looking at is the newspaper *Overseas Job Express (OJE)*, PO Box 22, Brighton BN1 6HX. This provides practical advice about working abroad and also lists vacancies around the world. Copies can be consulted at Jobcentres. *OJE* also operate a database of vacancies and job advertisements from employers worldwide.

EUROPE

Due to its proximity to Britain, and the existence of that ever-expanding body the European Community, Europe is the most prolific provider of temporary job possibilities. Since the beginning of 1993 and the creation of a single European market it has become much easier for UK citizens to look for work in EC countries. All EC nationals have the right to live and work in other member countries without a work permit.

It was hoped that from January 1993, the implementation of the European Economic Space agreement, would remove the need for work permits in non-EC countries. However, this legislation has been delayed and at the time of writing work permits are still required for most non-EC countries.

One outlet that can help with finding jobs in European countries is our own Jobcentre. They not only have leaflets concerning employment in all EC countries but they also have access to overseas vacancies on the *National Vacancy System (NATVACS)*. Ask at your local Jobcentre for details.

Another useful source of information is The Overseas Placing

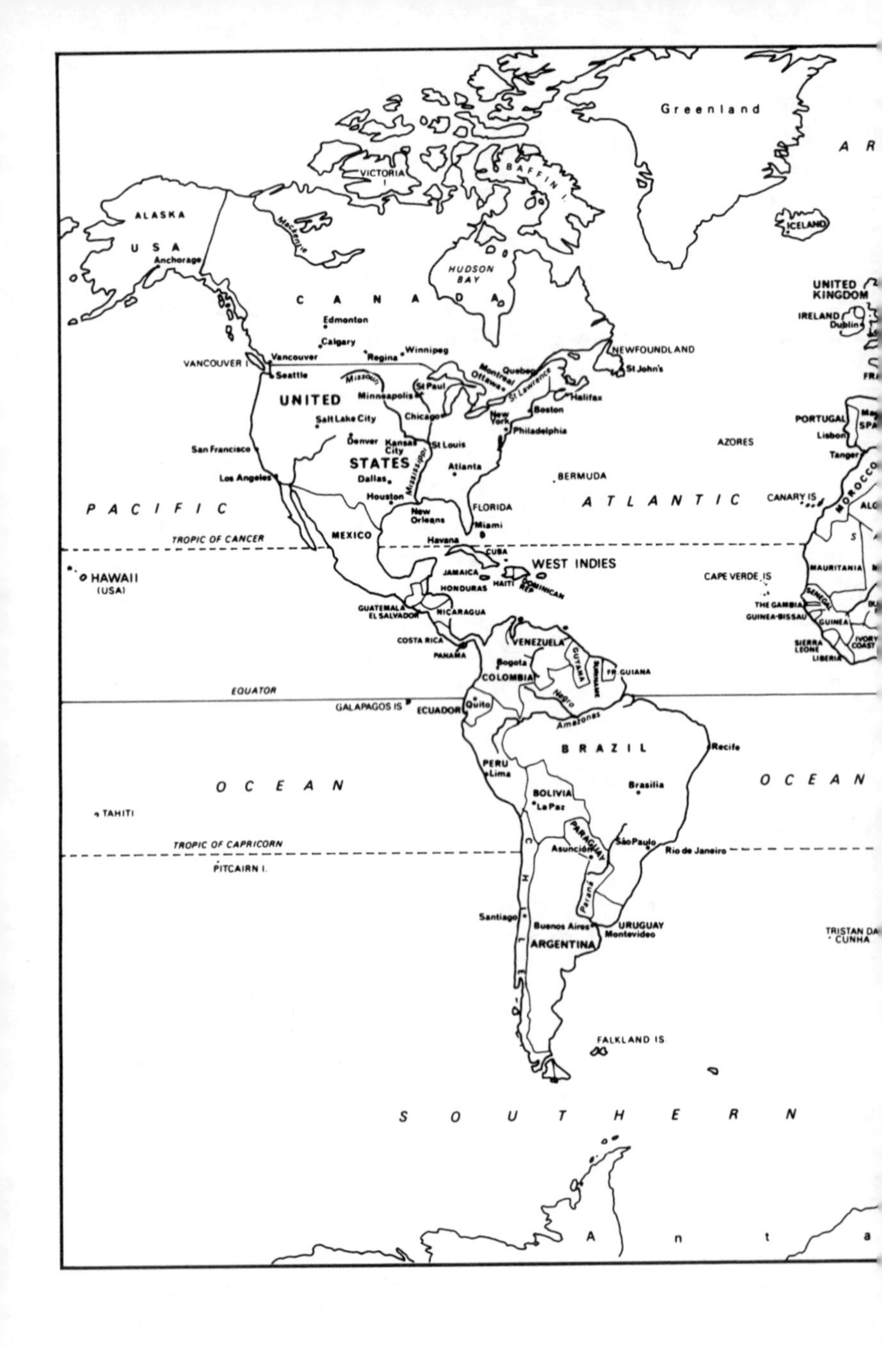

Fig. 3. Map of the world.

OCEAN
Siberia
RUSSIA
Yenisey
Lena
FINLAND
Helsinki
SWEDEN
St Petersburg
Stockholm
BALTIC REPUBLICS
Volga
Moscow
Sverdlovsk
Novosibirsk
Irtysh
Irkutsk
Amur
Berlin
Warsaw
POLAND
Kiev
UKRAINE
CZECH
GEORGIA
Volgograd
KAZAKHSTAN
MONGOLIA
ROMANIA
BLACK SEA
BULGARIA
Istanbul
Tbilisi
CASPIAN SEA
UZBEKISTAN
Tashkent
Vladivostok
Beijing
Ankara
TURKEY
Athens
GREECE
CHINA
Seoul
KOREA
JAPAN
Tokyo
Huanghe
Xi'an
Tehran
IRAN
Kabul
AFGHAN-ISTAN
Indus
IRAQ
Baghdad
SYRIA
ISRAEL
Jerusalem
JORDAN
TIBET
Wuhan
Shanghai
Yangtze
Kathmandu
NEPAL
PAKISTAN
Delhi
INDIA
LIBYA
EGYPT
Cairo
Nile
SAUDI ARABIA
OMAN
YEMEN PEOPLE'S DEM.REP
YEMEN ARAB REP
Dacca
BANGLADESH
BURMA
Hanoi
Hong Kong
TAIWAN
Bombay
ARABIAN SEA
THAI-LAND
Bangkok
LAOS
VIET-NAM
CHINA SEA
Manila
PHILIPPINES
CHAD
SUDAN
ETHIOPIA
Madras
ANDAMAN IS
SRI LANKA
NICOBAR IS
KAMPUCHEA
CENTRAL AFRICAN REP
SOMALIA
MALAYSIA
Kuala Lumpur
Singapore
SUMATRA
KENYA
UGANDA
CONGO
ZAÏRE
SEYCHELLES
NEW GUINEA
SOLOMON IS
TANZANIA
INDONESIA
JAVA
ANGOLA
ZAMBIA
MALAWI
COMORO IS
Darwin
INDIAN
Zambezi
S.W. AFRICA
(NAMIBIA)
ZIMBABWE
MOZAMBIQUE
BOTSWANA
MADAGASCAR (MALAGASY REP)
MAURITIUS
RÉUNION
Alice Springs
AUSTRALIA
Brisbane
SOUTH AFRICA
Durban
LESOTHO
Cape Town
OCEAN
Perth
Canberra
Sydney
Melbourne
TASMANIA
Auckland
Wellington
Christchurch
NEW ZEALAND
OCEAN
ctica

Unit (OPU), Steel City House, c/o Rockingham House, 123 West Street, Sheffield S1 4ER. They can provide information about specific countries and areas of employment.

Austria

Austrian Embassy, 18 Belgrave Mews West, London SW1X 5HU. Tel: (071) 235 3731.

Visa/work permit requirements

No visas are required for UK citizens who are visiting Austria for up to 6 months. Work permits are required for all types of work. These should be applied for before you travel to Austria and there are only a limited number available.

Length of stay permitted

Up to 6 months without the need for applying for a visa.

Types of temporary work available

Au pairs, camp couriers, chalet workers, farmworkers, hospitality industry.

Official recruitment agencies

The state run employment agency is Arbeitsamt. These are their regional offices:

Landesarbeitsamt für das Burgenland, Permayerstrasse 10, 7001 Eisenstadt.

Landesarbeitsamt für Karnten, Kumpfgasse 25, 9010 Klagenfurt.

Landesarbeitsamt für Oberosterreich, Gruberstrasse 63, 4010 Linz.

Landesarbeitsamt für Salzburg, Auerspergstrasse 67a, 5021 Salzburg.

Landesarbeitsamt für Tirol, Schopfstrasse 5, 8010 Innsbruck.

Landesarbeitsamt für Steiermark, Babenbergerstrasse 33, 8021 Graz.

Landesarbeitsamt für Vorarlburg, Rheinstrasse 32, 6901 Bregenz.

Landesarbeirsamt für Wein, Weihburggasse 30, 1011 Wien.

All letters sent to these offices must be written in German.

Prospective employers

Au pairs

Academy Au Pair Agency Ltd, Glenlea, Dulwich Common, London SE21 7ES.

Arbeitsgemeinschaft Auslands-Sozialdienst, Au-Pair-Vermittlung, Johannesgasse 16/1, 1010 Vienna, Austria.

Austrian Committee for International Educational Exchange, Au

Pair Department, Garnisongasse 7, 1090 Vienna, Austria.
Universal Care, Chester House, 9 Windsor End, Beaconsfield, Buckinghamshire HP9 2JJ.
Young Austria, Alpenstrasse 108a, A–5020 Salzburg, Austria.
Unlike other professions au pairs do not pay income tax or contribute to national health and social security schemes so it is vital that au pairs have their own private health insurance.

Camp couriers
See Chapter 4.

Hospitality
Alpenhotel Kaiser Franz Josef-Haus, Balthasar Sauper, A–9844 Heiligenblut, Austria.
Bladon Lines, Personnel Department, 56-58 Putney High Street, London SW15 1SF. Provides opportunities for chalet workers.
Hotel Feriengut-Gargellenhof, A–6787 Gargellen/Montafon, Vorarlberg, Austria.
Fernpass Hotel, A–6465 Post Nassereith, Tyrol, Austria.
Rotfluhhotel, A–6673 Haldensee, Seestrasse 5, Austria.

Other useful addresses
Austrian Committee for the International Exchange of Students (OKISTA), Turkenstrasse 4, A–1090 Vienna.

Temporary work rating
Good, but only if you have a solid working knowledge of German. The ski resorts are the most popular areas for temporary work but this naturally attracts the greatest number of workers. Unless you get in early in the season then it may be difficult to find a post. It could be worthwhile to look for work in some of the less popular areas — do not always follow the crowds.

Belgium

Belgian Embassy, 103 Eaton Square, London SW1W 9AB. Tel: (071) 235 5422.

Visa/work permit requirements
Visas and work permits are not required by UK citizens. However, people who are looking for work should report to the local Town Hall within eight days of their arrival in Belgium. The local authorities will then issue a matriculation card valid for at least three months. This will later be exchanged for an EC identity card

Fig. 4. Map of Europe.

on production of a confirmation of employment letter.

Length of stay permitted
Up to three months without applying for a **Residence Card**.

Types of temporary work available
Au pair, camp courier, hospitality.

Official recruitment agencies
(State run service for different areas)
Vlaamse Dienst voor Arbeidsbemiddeling (VDAB), Flanders.
Office de la Formation Professionelle de l'Emploi (FOREM), Wallonia.
Office Regional Bruxellois et de l'Emploi (BGDA/ORBEM), Brussels.
Nationwide offices for temporary work
Keizerslaan 11, 1000 Brussels. Tel: 02 514 57 00.
Rollewagenstraat 22, 1801 Vilvoorde. Tel: 02 252 20 25.
Jezusstraat 5–7, 2000 Antwerpen. Tel: 03 232 98 60.
Spanjaardstraat 17, 8000 Brugge. Tel: 050 44 04 70.
Pensmarkt 2, 9000 Gent. Tel: 091 24 09 20.
Thonissenlaan 47, 3500 Hasselt. Tel: 011 22 11 77.
Beheerstraat 68, 8500 Kortrijk. Tel: 056 20 30 79.
De Merodelei 86, 2300 Turnhout. Tel: 014 42 27 1.
Rue de la Province 22, 4020 Liège. Tel: 041 41 03 10.
Rue de Bruxelles 35b, 4800 Verviers. Tel: 087 22 54 00.
Rue Borgnet 14, 5000 Namur. Tel: 081 22 30 12.
Rue de Montignies 36, 6000 Charleroi. Tel: 071 31 74 45.

Other useful addresses
Federation of Recruitment and Employment Services Limited (FRES), 36–38 Mortimer Street, London W1N 7RB.
CEPEC Recruitment Guide, CEPEC Limited, 67 Jermyn Street, London SW1Y 6NY. Tel: (071) 930 0322.
Commission of the European Communities, Recruitment Unit–COM/A/724, rue de la Loi 200, 1049 Brussels. Tel: 02 235 11 11.
Fonds des Accidents du Travail, Rue du Trone 1000, 1050 Brussels. Tel: 02 506 84 11. To be contacted in the event of an accident at work.
Publicitas Ltd, 525 Fulham Road, London SW6. Tel: (071) 385 7723. Can place job advertisements in Belgian newspapers.
Weekly magazine for job vacancies — *The Bulletin*, Avenue Molière, 329, 1060 Brussels. Tel: 02 343 99 09.

Prospective employers

Au pairs

The Windrose, Avenue des Demineurs la, 1090 Brussels. Tel: 02 425 32 33/02 425 40 71.

Stuvan, Vierwindenlaan 7, 1810 Wemmel. Tel: 02 460 33 95.

Students Abroad Ltd, 11 Milton View, Hitchin, Herts SG4 0QD. Tel: (0462) 438909.

Couriers

See Chapter 4.

Hospitality

Hotel des Broyères, 13 rte de Houffalize, 5980 La Roche en Ardenne.

Hotel de la Poste, Place St. Arnould 1, 6830 Bouillon. Tel: 061 466506.

Jules Ricail, 5 Rue de la Gendarmerie, 5570 Beauraing.

Temporary work rating

Good, but a knowledge of French would greatly help prospective employees find work. Belgium has a solid tourist income and this may be one of the best areas for the temporary worker.

Bulgaria

Bulgarian Embassy, 186 Queen's Gate, London SW7 5HL. Tel: (071) 584 9400.

Visa/work permit requirements

UK citizens require visas to work in Bulgaria.

Length of stay permitted

Varies according to the job.

Types of temporary work available

Limited openings for camp couriers and voluntary work.

Prospective employers

Camp couriers

Crystal Holidays, Crystal House, The Courtyard, Arlington Road, Surbiton, Surrey KT6 6BW. Tel: (081) 390 8737.

Ski Ardmore, 11–15 High Street, Marlow, Buckinghamshire SL7 1AU. Tel: (0628) 89060.

Voluntary work

ARGO-M, Boulevard Stamboliski 2A, Sofia 100, Bulgaria. Run work camps undertaking a variety of community projects.

Temporary work rating

Poor. The only real opportunities are with official organisations and these are extremely limited.

Cyprus

Cyprus High Commission, 93 Park Street, London W1Y 4ET. Tel: (071) 499 8272.

Visa/work permit requirements

Visas and work permits are required for UK citizens. These are often difficult to obtain for employment and the Cypriot High Commissioner sums up the situation: 'To obtain a work permit you should first find an employer willing to offer you a job in Cyprus, your employer should then apply for a work permit on your behalf. Applications for work permits are very carefully scrutinised and approval is only given in rare cases when the application is shown to be in the public interest'.

Types of temporary work available

Officially, not much. However, there is a thriving tourist industry and also a variety of fruit-picking, if you are prepared to take the risk of working illegally.

Official recruitment agencies and other useful addresses

Job Centre Employment Agency, 37 Annis Komnenis Street, Office 6, Nicosia. Tel: 02 457045.

Job Hunters, 117 Athalassa Avenue, Dassoupolis. Tel: 02 420103.

Ministry of the Interior, Department of Aliens and Immigration, D. Sevris Avenue, Nicosia. Tel: 02 303138.

Temporary work rating

Poor. The only real possibilities are for people who are in Cyprus and with an eye to the main chance.

Czech Republic

Czech Republic Embassy, 25 Kensington Palace Gardens, London W8 4QY. Tel: (071) 229 1255.

Visa/work permit requirements

UK citizens can stay in the Czech Republic for six months without a visa. However, for people looking for work it is necessary to obtain a temporary residence permit and also a work permit. The residence permit should be applied for through the Czech Republic Embassy. You can then apply for a work permit once you have found a job. These are issued by the District Labour Offices.

Types of temporary work available

Temporary teaching and voluntary work are the most hopeful openings.

Useful addresses

Urad prace hl.m. Prathy, Zborovska 5, 150 00 Praha 5, Czech Republic. Employment advice.

Brit-Pol Health Care Foundation, Gerrard House, Suite 14, Worthing Road, East Preston, West Sussex BN16 1AW. Tel: (0903) 859222. An organisation which provides teachers to work on summer camps in the Czech Republic. Teachers aged from 20–50 are wanted for three weeks in July and August.

Klub Maldych Cestovatelu (KMC), Malostranske nabrezil, 118 00 Prague 1. Volunteers for international work camps engaged in conservation, construction and agricultural work.

Temporary work rating

Moderate — there are no prohibitively strict regulations to stop foreigners taking up work in the Czech Republic but it will take equal measures of a knowledge of the language and determination in order to find a temporary job in this fledgling country.

Denmark

Danish Embassy, 55 Sloane Street, London SW1X 9SR. Tel: (071) 235 1255.

Visa/work permit requirements

UK citizens are entitled to look for employment for the first three months of their stay in Denmark. Once a job has been found a residence permit will be issued. This is done by writing to: The Directorate of Aliens, Absalonsgade 9, 1658 Copenhagen V. Tel: 31 22 08 77. Application must be made at least two weeks before your three months free stay has expired.

Types of temporary work available

Au pair, camp couriers, conservation, farm work, fruit-picking and hospitality.

Official recruitment agencies

The major Labour Exchanges in Denmark (all run by the Government).

AF–Kontoret, Norregade 44, 7400 Herning, Denmark. Tel: 010 45 97 12 25 88.

AF–Konteret, Ringgade 253, PO Box 49, 6400 Sonderborg, Denmark. Tel: 010 45 74 42 33 41.

AF–Kontoret, Teglvaerksgade 4, PO Box 510, 6701 Esbjerg, Denmark. Tel: 010 45 75 12 33 44.

AF–Kontoret, Sonderbrogade 34, 7100 Vejle, Denmark. Tel: 010 45 75 82 04 99.

AF–Kontoret, Norreport 15, PO Box 399, 8100 Aarhus C, Denmark. Tel: 010 45 86 13 34 22.

AF–Kontoret, Faelledvej 3, PO Box 20, 8800 Viborg, Denmark. Tel: 010 45 86 62 35 88.

AF–Kontoret, Kjellerupgade 12, PO Box 830, 9100 Aalborg, Denmark. Tel: 010 45 98 16 90 00.

AF–Kontoret, Gabensvej 116, PO Box 179, 4800 Nykobing Falster, Denmark. Tel: 010 45 54 85 15 55.

AF–Kontoret, Minervavej 1, PO Box 119, 3700 Ronne, Denmark. Tel: 010 45 56 95 30 33.

AF–Kontoret, Smedelundsgade 5, PO Box 60, 4300 Holbaek, Denmark.

AF–Kontoret, Helsinggorsdgade 10, PO Box 263, 3400 Hillerod, Denmark. Tel: 010 45 42 26 54 22.

AF–Kontoret, Jernbanegade 12, 4000 Roskilde, Denmark. Tel: 010 45 42 35 22 01.

AF–Kontoret, Tondergade 14, 1752 Copenhagen V, Denmark. Tel: 010 45 31 21 45 11.

AF–Kontoret, Dannebrosgade 3, 5000 Odense C, Denmark. Tel: 010 45 66 11 77 70.

Private agencies

Royal Service Appointments, 28B Norregade, 1165 Copenhagen, Denmark. Tel: 010 13 30 99/13 90 83. Supply cleaners and dishwashers to several Copenhagen hotels.

Adia, N. Volgade 82, Copenhagen, Denmark.

Manpower, Vesterbrogade 12–14, Copenhagen, Denmark.

Western Service, Kobmagergade 54, Copenhagen, Denmark.

Prospective employers

Au pairs

Langtrain International, Torquay Road, Foxrock, Dublin 18, Ireland. Tel: 1 289 3876.

Universal Care, Chester House, 9 Windsor Road, Beaconsfield, Bucks HP9 2JJ. Tel: (0494) 678811.

Farmwork

International Farm Experience Programme, YFC Centre, National Agricultural Centre, Kenilworth, Warwickshire CV8 2LG. Tel: (0203) 696584. Work experience on farms for periods of 3–12 months.

Vi Hjaelper Hinanden, Inga Nielsen, Asenvej 35, 9881 Bindslev. Tel: 010 98 93 86 07. Voluntary workers to help on organic farms.

Fruit-picking

Graevlerupgaard Frugtplantage, Egsgyden 38, Horne, 5600 Faborg. Tel: 010 62 60 22 31. Fruit pickers needed to pick strawberries during June and July.

Orbaekgard Frugtplantage, Odensevej 28, 5853 Orbaek. Tel: 010 65 33 12 57. Strawberry picking in July and cherry picking in August.

Hospitality

In the words of the Danish Embassy: 'Our experience is that the foreigners who do find a job in Denmark, do it by asking around and looking up the employers on their own initiative. This applies especially for the hotel and restaurant trade'.

Other useful addresses

Folkeregisteret (The National Register), Dahlerupsgade 6, 1640 Copenhagen V. Tel: 010 33 66 33 66. Anyone who is working in Denmark requires a personal code number and this can be applied for at this address. To obtain a **personal code number** you will need to have a residence/labour permit and also a permanent address —a youth hostel or hotel address will not suffice.

Youth Information Copenhagen, Radhusstraede 13, DK 1466 Copenhagen K. They publish a useful booklet for temporary workers entitled *Working in Denmark*.

Frank L. Crane Ltd, 5–15 Cromer Street, Gray's Inn Road, London WC1H 8LS. Can place job advertisements in Danish newspapers.

Ministry for Labour, Arbejdsministeriet, Laksgade 19, DK–1603 Copenhagen K, Denmark. Tel: 010 45 33 92 59 00. General employment information.

Studentformidlingen, Svanevej 22, St, 2400 Copenhagen NV. Tel:

010 38 33 00 21. The student branch of the Danish employment service. This branch should be visited in person.

International Committee of Students, DIS, Skindergade 36, DK–1159 Copenhagen K, Denmark. Tel: 010 45 33 11 11 00.

Temporary work rating

Good. Although it is useful to have a knowledge of Danish this is not essential as most people in Denmark speak English. There are possibilities in hospitality (many people work in the ubiquitous McDonalds) and also in fruit-picking and fish processing. One down side is that it is expensive to live in Denmark so it is preferable to find paid employment as soon as possible if you do not want your funds to rapidly diminish.

Finland

Finnish Embassy, 38 Chesham Place, London SW1X 8HW. Tel: (071) 235 9531.

Visa/work permit requirements

No visa is required for UK citizens but a work permit is still required. This can only be applied for once you have a written job offer. This should then be sent to the Finnish Embassy. Processing takes approximately four weeks.

Length of stay permitted

Usually three months.

Types of temporary work available

Au pair, domestic, farm work, hospitality and voluntary work.

Employment opportunities

International Trainee Exchanges.

This is a popular programme, promoted by the Ministry of Labour and administered in Britain through the Central Bureau, Seymour Mews House, London W1H 9PE. Potential trainees should have studied for a minimum of one year, preferably in the field of commerce, economics, agriculture, forestry or tourism. Placements are initially for three months but this is frequently extended. Trainees are paid the same as Finnish workers doing equivalent jobs.

Family stays

Also run by the Ministry of Labour this is a programme for 18–23-year-olds, who spend up to three months with a Finnish family, working either in their home or on their farm. Accommodation and food is provided as well as approximately £30 a week pocket money. Finnish Family Programme, Centre for International Mobility, PB 343, 00531 Helsinki, Finland. Tel: 0 774 77033.

Prospective employers

Farmwork

International Farm Experience Programme, YFC Centre, National Agricultural Centre, Stoneleigh Park, Kenilworth, Warwickshire CV8 2LG. Tel: (0203) 696584.

Voluntary work

Valamo Monastery, 79850 Uusi-Valamo, Finland. Tel: 72 61911. Large numbers of volunteers spend a few weeks helping at the monastery each year.

Work camps

KVT, Rauhanasema, Veturitori, 00520 Helsinki 52, Finland.

Useful addresses

The Finnish Centre for International Trainee Exchange Programmes, PO Box 343, SF–00531 Helsinki, Finland.

Frank L. Crane Limited, 5/15 Cromer Street, Gray's Inn Road, London WC1H 8LS. Can place job advertisements in Finnish newspapers.

Temporary work rating

Moderate. Since a work permit is still required this could make the situation more difficult. Official placement schemes offer the best bet for short-term employment and experience of the Finnish way of life.

France

French Embassy, 22 Wilton Crescent, London SW1X 8SB. Tel: (071) 235 8080.

Visa/work permit requirements

UK citizens require only a valid passport to enter France to look for work. Prospective employees can spend up to three months in France looking for work. When a job has been found a carte de séjour (a residence permit) should be applied for from the mairie (town hall) or prefecture of your place of residence. This will be granted on production of a valid passport, birth certificate (translated into French — get it done before you go), three passport photographs, proof of accommodation and proof of employment.

Length of stay permitted
Indefinite once work has been found.

Types of temporary work available
Au pair, archaeology, camp couriers, conservation, fruit-picking, hospitality (including work in ski resorts), labouring, teaching, voluntary work, and work camps. France is one of the best possibilities for temporary work and anyone who can speak French should be able to find some kind of employment.

Official recruitment agencies
The national employment agency is the **Agence Nationale pour l'Emploi (ANPE)**. This is the equivalent of Jobcentres in the UK and there are over 650 branches throughout the country. They advertise a wide range of jobs and this is the best starting point for job seekers who have just arrived in France. There are special seasonal offices in areas where fruit-picking and other seasonal work is prevalent and these are always worth a visit. The head office of ANPE is at Le Galilée, 4 rue Galilée, 93198 Noisy-le-Grand, France. They can provide a list of all regional offices.

Another useful group of agencies are the **Centres d'Information et de Documentation Jeunesse (CIJ)**. There are 26 of them throughout France and they not only provide information regarding employment but they can also help with accommodation for temporary workers and legal rights. The head office is, Centre d'Information Jeunesse, 101 Quai Branly, 75740 Paris Cedex, France. When looking for work the offices have to be approached in person but if you send four International Reply Coupons to the head office they will send some invaluable leaflets covering seasonal work and also employment regulations.

One regional office of CIJ is the Provence-Alpes branch. This has a number of vacancies for people interested in working in one of the ski resorts.

Similar to the CIJs are the **Centres Régional des Oeuvres Universitaires et Scolaires**. They are located in French university towns and they operate a service designed specifically to find students holiday jobs — **Le Service de Liaison Etudiante**. They generally insist that people are studying in France but they have been known to help people who managed to pass as students.

There are numerous private job agencies in France and these are best for temporary office jobs. Lists of individual agencies can be found in the *Yellow Pages* of all major French towns.

Types of work and prospective employers

Au pairs

France has a detailed procedure for au pair work and people aged between 18 and 30 can work as au pairs for at least three months but usually no longer than 12 months (although this can sometimes be extended to 18 months).

Once a job has been found it is up to the organisation who arranged the post or the French host family to obtain an **Accord de placement au pair d'un stagiaire aide-familial** (mother's help work contract). This is done through the Direction Departementale du Travail et de l'Emploi (Paris office, Service de la Main-d'Oeuvre Etrangère, 80 rue de la Croix-Nivert, 75732 Paris Cedex 15, France). Once the formalities have been dealt with a copy will be sent to the au pair. When he/she arrives in France this contract should be produced together with a valid passport and a certificate of enrolment at a school specialising in teaching English to foreign students. After this the appropriate visa will be issued.

Au pair organisations in France

Accueil Familial des Jeunes Etrangers, 23 rue du Cherche-Midi, 75006 Paris, France.

Comité Parisien de l'Association Catholique des Services de Jeunesse Feminine, 65 rue Monsieur le Prince, 75006 Paris, France.

Alliance Française, 101 Boulevard Raspail, 75006 Paris, France.

Inter-Séjours, 179 rue de Courcelles, 75017 Paris, France.

Séjours Internationaux Linguistiques et Culturels, 32 Rempart de l'Est, 16022 Angoulême Cedex, France.

Au pair organisations in the UK

Academy Au Pair Agency Limited, Glenlea, Dulwich Common, London SW21 7ES. Tel: (081) 299 4599.

Anglo Pair Agency, 40 Wavertree Road, Streatham Hill, London SW2 3SP. Tel: (081) 674 3605.

Just the Job Employment Agency, 8 Musters Road, West Bridgford, Nottingham NG2 5PL. Tel: (0602) 813224.

Langtrain International, Torquay Road, Foxrock, Dublin 18, Ireland. Tel: 1 289 3876.

Students Abroad, 11 Milton View, Hitchin, Herts SG4 0QD. Tel: (0462) 438909.

Camp Couriers

See Chapter 4 for general organisations.

Charisma Holidays, Bethel House, Heronsgate Road, Chorleywood, Herts WD3 5BB. Tel: (0923) 284235.

Freedom of France, Alton Court, Penyard Lane (878), Ross-on-Wye, Herefordshire HR9 5NR. Tel: (0989) 767833.

French Country Camping, 126 Hempstead Road, Kings Langley, Herts WD4 8AL. Tel: (0923) 261316.

French Life Motoring Holidays, 26 Church Road, Horsforth, Leeds LS18 5LG. Tel: (0532) 390077.

Keycamp Holidays, 92–96 Lind Road, Sutton, Surrey SM1 4PL. Tel: (081) 395 8170.

Mark Warner, 20 Kensington Church Street, London W8 4EP. Tel: (071) 937 4822.

Matthews Holidays, 8 Bishopmead Parade, East Horsley, Leatherhead, Surrey KT24 6RP.

NSS Riviera Holidays, 199 Marlborough Avenue, Hull HU15 3LG.

Sandpiper Camping Holidays Limited, Sandpiper House, 19 Fairmile Avenue, Cobham, Surrey KT11 2JA.

School World, The Coach House, Tyn-y-Coed Place, Roath Park, Cardiff CF2 4TX. Tel: (0222) 470077.

Seasun School Tours, Seasun House, 4 East Street, Colchester, Essex CO1 2XW.

Simply Travel Limited, 8 Chiswick Terrace, Acton Lane, London W4 5LY. Tel: (081) 995 3883.

Susi Madron's Cycling for Softies, 2 & 4 Birch Polygon, Rusholme, Manchester M14 5HX. Tel: (061) 248 8282.

Westents Limited, 88 New North Road, Huddersfield, West Yorkshire HD1 5NE. Tel: (0484) 424455.

Farm work

Looking at the shelves of any wine shop it is easy to deduce that the most common form of agricultural work for temporary workers in France is grape-picking. It is hard, dirty, gruelling work, but in the long run more rewarding than sitting behind a desk all day. Wages and conditions can vary considerably, sometimes between adjacent vineyards, and before starting work somewhere it is a good idea to try and talk to someone who has already been there.

Due to the recession there is now more competition for grape-picking work than there was ten years ago so you will need to go about your job search with determination and patience. The grape harvest usually begins in late September or early October but this varies according to the region and the weather.

There are ANPE offices in all wine producing areas and these would be a good starting point when looking for work:

- **Alsace**

ANPE, 1mm. Wilson, 3 rue Sarrelouis, 67081 Strasbourg.

- **Beaujolais**

ANPE, 42 rue Paul Bert, 69400 Villefranche-sur-Saône. Tel: 74 65 19 99.

- **Bordeaux**

ANPE, 1 Terrasse du Front du Médoc, 33077 Bordeaux. Tel: 56 90 92 92.

ANPE, 108 rue du Président Carnot, BP 196, 33504 Libourne. Tel: 5751 18 08.

ANPE, 13 cours des Fosses, 33210 Langon. Tel: 56 62 34 88.

ANPE, 29 rue Ferdinand Buisson, BP 57, 33250, Pauillac. Tel: 56 59 07 51.

ANPE, 17 rue St. Simon, BP 80, 33390 Blaye. Tel: 57 42 13 14.

- **Burgundy**

ANPE, 71 rue Jean-Mace, BP 20, 71031 Mâcon. Tel: 85 38 78 22.

ANPE, 6 Boulevard St. Jacques, BP 115, 21203 Beaune. Tel: 80 24 60 00.

ANPE, 7 rue des Corroyeurs, BP 1504, 21033 Dijon. Tel: 80 43 17 67.

- **Champagne**

ANPE, 57 rue de Talleyrand, 51087 Reims Cedex.

ANPE, 11 rue Jean Moet, BP 502, 51331 Epernay. Tel: 26 51 01 33.

- **Languedoc-Roussillon**

ANPE, 43 Avenue Pont Juvenal, 34000 Montpellier.

- **Loire**

ANPE, Champ Girault, 9 rue du Docteur Herpin, BP 2510, 370265 Tours. Tel: 47 20 49 14.

ANPE, Square Lafayette, BP 845, 49000 Angers. Tel: 41 88 56 25.

Even if one ANPE paints a particularly gloomy picture about getting a picking job it is worth persevering since some people tend to get fed up with picking jobs fairly quickly and there are new vacancies arising on a daily basis. If you want to visit vineyards personally one way to get addresses is to look at some labels of wine produced in the area you want to visit and then write directly to the producer.

There are also specific recruiting agencies for prospective pickers who are already in France. Two of these are:

The Centre de Documentation et d'Information Rurale, 92 rue du Dessous-des-Berges, 75013 Paris, France. Tel: 45 83 04 92.

Jeunesse et Reconstruction, 10 rue de Trevise, 75009 Paris, France. Tel: 47 70 15 88.

In addition to grape-picking there is also temporary work for harvesting apples, apricots, cherries, hay, maize, melons, peaches, pears, plums, raspberries, strawberries and tomatoes. Much of this work can be found between May and November in the Ardèche, Hérault, Drôme and Gers regions.

Hospitality

This is an area rich in openings for people who have some experience in the hospitality industry and can speak passable French — it is no good looking for a job as a waiter/waitress if you are going to have to ask the customers to speak slowly and loudly.

One recent addition to the hospitality scene in France is of course Euro Disney. The organisation employs 12,000 permanent staff but at any one time they need 5,000 temporary workers in a variety of jobs ranging from attraction hosts to cleaners. The minimum period of work for temporary workers is two months between April and October and the maximum length of employment is usually six months. Workers are kept on the go all the time and the organisation expects high standards from its employees. People working with the public are expected to be helpful and cheerful at all times — after a few weeks you may be afraid that the ever-present Disney-grin is beginning to crack your face. Budding Plutos and Mickey Mice can be reassured that costumes are provided. People interested in working at Euro Disney should write to, Euro Disney, Casting Center, BP 110, 77777 Marne la Vallée, France.

Other hospitality possibilities UK based

People with hospitality experience wishing to apply for a temporary job in a French hotel or restaurant should write to, The British Hotel, Restaurant and Caterer Association, 13 Cork Street, London W1X 2BH. Tel: (071) 499 6641.

Other British organisations who employ hospitality staff to work in France include:

Acorn Venture, 137 Worcester Road, Hagley, Stourbridge, West Midlands DY9 0NM. Tel: (0562) 882151. Experienced catering staff required.

Alpotels Agency, PO Box 388, London SW1X 8LX. Interview workers for jobs in French hotels.

Bladon Lines Travel, 56–58 Putney High Street, London SW15 1SF. Tel: (081) 785 2200.

Campus Centres Limited, Llangarron, Near Ross-on-Wye, Herefordshire HR9 6P6. Tel: (0989) 770701.

Crystal Holidays, Crystal House, The Courtyard, Arlington Road, Surbiton, Surrey KT6 6BW. Tel: (081) 390 8737. Chalet staff required to work at French ski resorts.

Flot'Home UK/Barge France, 25 Kingswood Creek, Wraybury, Staines, Middlesex. Chefs required to work on holiday barges on French canals.

Lotus Supertravel, Alpine Operations Department, Mobbs Court, 2 Jacob Street, London SE1 2BL. Tel: (071) 962 9933. A wide range of staff required to work in French ski resorts.

PGL Young Adventure Limited, Alton Court, Penyard Lane (878), Ross-on-Wye, Herefordshire HR9 5NR. Hospitality staff required to work at adventure holiday centres around France.

Skibound, Olivier House, 18 Marine Parade, Brighton, East Sussex BN2 1TL. A variety of hospitality staff required to work in French ski resorts.

Addresses in France

Most of the posts at the following addresses are for a variety of hospitality positions. These can change from season to season so a preliminary letter enquiring what posts are available would be a good idea. It is best to do this a few months before you hope to begin work — six months would not be unreasonable in some cases.

With the current high levels of unemployment in France one of the most likely jobs for the temporary job seeker is that of a washer-up (plongeur) as it is one of the worst jobs and many nationals will not even consider it. Even if you do draw a blank with these addresses it is worth keeping them in mind and visiting them in person when you get to France. Hospitality personnel change more frequently than the weather and being on the spot is the best way to land a job.

Auberge du Col, Curebourse, 15800 Vic-Sur-Cere, France. Tel: 71 47 51 71.

Garden Beach Hôtel, 15–17 Bd. Baudoin, 06160 Juan les Pins, France. Tel: 93 67 25 25.

Grand Hôtel du Parc, 47 Avenue Jean Monestier, 48400 Florac, France.

Hôtel Beauséjour, 15800 Vic-Sur-Cere, France.

Hôtel du Bras-Breau, 22 Rue Grande, 77630 Barbizon, France.

Hôtel Château de l'Aubrière, 37390 la Membrolle-sur-Choisille, France.

Hôtel International Royal Splendid, 18 Avenue Charles de Gaulle, 73100 Aix-les-Bains, France. Tel: 79 88 00 59.

Hôtel Mireille, 2 Place St. Pierre, 13200 Arles en Provence, France.

Hôtel Moulin des Pommerats, 89210 Venizy-St-Lorentin, France. Tel: 86 35 08 04.

Hôtel Terrasse Fleurie, 65170 Saint-Lary-Soulan, France. Tel: 62940 26.

Hostellerie le Beffroi, BP 85, 84110 Vaison la Romaine, Provence, France.

Restaurant la Mijotière, Pont de Sables (Fourques), Lot-et-Garonne, France.

Sarl Hôtel Poste et Golfe, 31110 Luchou, France.

UK Overseas Handling Limited, Le Plein Soleil, 73550 Meribel-Mottaret, France. Tel: 33 79 00 42 91.

Voluntary work

Archaeology

France has a large number of opportunities for budding archaeologists (or even just enthusiastic volunteers who want to do something a bit different) at archaeological digs.

Association de Recherches et d'Etudes d'Histoire Rurale, Serge Grappin, Maison du Patrimoine, 21190 Saint-Roman, France. Volunteers required to work on digs in the Burgundy village of Saint-Roman.

Asssociation pour le Développement de l'Archéologie Urbaine à Chartres, 16 rue Sainte Pierre, 28000 Chartres, France. Volunteers required for digs in Chartres.

Cercle Archéologique de Bray/Seine, Claude and Daniel Mordant, rue du Tour de l'Eglise, Dannemoine, 89700 Tonnerre, France. volunteers required for digs at Grisy and Balloy.

Groupe Archéologique du Mémontois, Louis Rousel, Directeur des Fouilles, 52 rue des Forges, 21000 Dijon. Volunteers required for digs at Malain on the Côte d'Or.

Laboratoire d'Anthropologie Préhistorique, Université de Rennes I, Campus de Beaulieu, 35042 Rennes Cedex, France. Volunteers required for digs throughout Brittany.

Professor John Collis, Department of Archaeology, Sheffield University, Sheffield, S10 2TN. Tel: (0742) 78555. Takes volunteers to work on farm settlements in the Clermont Ferrand region.

Musée des Sciences Naturelles et d'Archéologie, Service Archéologique du Musée de la Chartreuse, Pierre Demolon, Conservateur de Musée, 191 rue St-Albin, 59500 Douai, France. Volunteers required for digs in Douai.

Musée National d'Histoire Naturelle, Laboratorie de Préhistoire, Institut de Paléontologie Humaine, Professeur Henry de Lumley, 1 rue René Panhard, 75013 Paris, France. Volunteers required for digs throughout south east and south west France.

Service Archéologique-Ville d'Arras, Alain Jacques, 22 rue Paul Doumer, 62000 Arras, France. Volunteers required for digs in Arras.

Unité de Recherche Archéologique, The Director, No 12, Centre National de la Recherche Scientifique, 3 rue Michelet, 75006 Paris, France. Volunteers required for digs in the Vallée de l'Aisne.

Université du Maine, Annie Renoux, Département d'Histoire, Avenue Olivier Messiaen, BP 535, 72017 Le Mans, France. Volunteers required for digs at Chavot, Epernay and Champagne.

Conservation

Les Alpes de Lumière, Prieure de Salagon, Mane, 04300 Forcalquier, France. Organises renovation projects throughout Haute-Provence.

Association Chantiers Histoire et Architecture Medievales (CHAM), 5 & 7 rue Guilleminot, 75014 Paris, France. Work restoring historic French medieval buildings and monuments.

Association le Mat, le Viel Audon, Balazuc, 07120 Ruoms, France. Volunteers required to restore a village in the Ardèche.

Association pour la Participation a l'Action Régionale (APARE), 41 cours Jean Jaures, 84000 Avignon, France. Run a range of restorative programmes throughout Provence aimed at protecting the region's environment and heritage.

Centre Permanent d'Initiation à la Forêt Provençale, Hôtel de Ville, Chemin du Loubatas, 13860 Peyolles, France. Organise work camps to teach volunteers the dangers of forest fires in the south of France.

Club du Vieux Manoir, 10 rue de la Cossonnérie, 75001 Paris, France. Specifically for young people, this organisation helps restore monuments and sites all over France.

Les Compagnons du Cap, Pratcoustals, Arphy, 30120 Le Vigan, France. Use volunteers to help restore the abandoned village of Pratcoustals.

Etudes et Chantiers International, 33 rue Campagne Première, 75014 Paris, France. Organise the redevelopment of rural communities.

Jeunesse et Reconstruction, 10 rue de Trévise, 75009 Paris, France. Tel: 1 47 70 15 88. Help redevelop small rural communities.

The Montauriol Trust, Le Berger, 11410 Montauriol, Aude, France. Tel: 68 60 34 30. Use volunteers to help restore buildings and houses in the Aude region.

Pierres Sèches en Vaucluse, La Cornette, 84800 Saumane, France. Organise work camps to teach drystone-walling techniques.

Restanques et Murets de Venasque, Mairie, 84210 Venaaque, France. Run work camps involved in environmental management and the restoration of monuments.

Solidarités Jeunesses, 38 rue du Faubourg St. Denis, 75010 Paris, France. Run projects to restore old mills and buildings.

Work camps

Centre de la Formation de la Jeunesse du Quart Monde, 29 rue du Stade, Champeaux, 77720 Mormant, France. Work camps in aid of helping the poor and disadvantaged, involving construction, carpentry, electrical installation, painting, gardening, office work and cooking.

Chantiers de Jeunes Provence-Côte d'Azur, 7 Avenue Pierre de Coubertin, 06150 Cannes la Bocca, France. Work camps geared particularly towards protection of the environment.

Collège Lycée Cevenol International, Camp International de Travail, 43400 Le Chambon sur Lignon, France. Tel: 71 59 72 52. A work camp to help restore and maintain an international school in the Massif Central.

Concordia, 38 rue du Faubourg St. Denis, 75010 Paris, France. (Apply through the UK office, 8 Brunswick Place, Hove, East Sussex BN3 1ET. Tel: (0273) 772086). Work camps throughout France, concentrating on environmental and restoration work.

International Movement ATD Fourth World, 107 Avenue du Général Leclerc, 5480 Pierrelaye, France. Volunteers required to help build an international centre at Mery Sur Oise.

Service Civil International, 2 rue Eugène Fournière, 75018 Paris, France. International work camps are organised throughout France, with the emphasis on international reconciliation through work projects.

Other useful addresses

French Publishing Group, 171 Fleet Street, London EC4. Tel: (071) 353 4418. Can place job advertisements in French newspapers.

Accueil des Jeunes en France, 12 rue des Barres, 75004 Paris, France. Youth and student information (correspondence).

Temporary work rating

Very good. France has a number of varied employment opportunities and it is accepted that people from the UK will want to work in France. But this does not mean that you can just hop onto a ferry and fall into a job on the other side. You should identify what type of work you want and then make sure you are qualified for it and willing to stick at it once you are there. One important factor is an ability to speak at least some French. It is a fallacy to think that everyone in France speaks English — they don't.

Germany

German Embassy, 23 Belgrave Square, London SW1X 8PZ. Tel: (071) 235 5033.

Visa/work permit requirements

No work permit or visa is required for UK citizens. As soon as employment is found (but not later than three months after arrival in the country) you should apply for a residence permit (aufenthaltserlaubnis) from the local Aliens Authority (Ausländeramt). If you have not found employment after three months you will not be able to apply for a residence permit.

Length of stay permitted

Three months while looking for work. Indefinite once work has been found.

Types of temporary work available

Au pair, camp couriers, farm work, fruit-picking, hospitality and voluntary work.

Official recruitment agencies

The national employment office in Germany is the **Arbeitsamt** which is like Britain's Jobcentres and can be used in the same way. This is a useful starting point for people in Germany.

Another alternative is to apply to the official government labour agency, **Zentralstelle für Arbeitsvermittlung**, Feuerbachstrasse 42–46, 6000 Frankfurt am Main, Germany. Tel: 01049 69 7111 0. They can arrange summer jobs in hospitality and agriculture. Applicants should be over 18 and be able to speak German. Applications should include nationality, date of birth, previous experience and current occupation.

Prospective employers

Au pairs

Anglia Agency, 70 Southsea Avenue, Leigh-on-Sea, Essex. Tel: (081) 299 4599.

Avalon Agency, Thursley House, 53 Station Road, Shalford, Guildford, Surrey GU4 8HA. Tel: (0483) 63640.

German Catholic Social Centre, Haus Lioba, 40 Exeter Road, London NW2 4SB. Tel: (081) 452 8566.

Jolaine Agency, 18 Escot Way, Barnet, Herts EN5 3AN. Tel: (081) 449 1334.

Langtrain International, Torquay Road, Foxrock, Dublin 18, Ireland. Tel: 1 289 3876.

Verein für Internationale Jugendarbeit. Affiliated to the World Young Women's Association, Employment Service, 39 Craven Road, London W2 3RY. Tel: (071) 723 0216.

Camp couriers

See Chapter 4.

Farm work

Since Germany's farms tend to be highly mechanised there are less opportunities here than in some other European countries. There are some jobs for grape-pickers during the grape harvest, which takes place in the west of the country during late October and early November. For organised farm work:

International Farm Experience Programme YFC Centre, National Agricultural Centre, Stoneleigh Park, Kenilworth, Warwickshire CV8 2LG. Tel: (0203) 696584.

Willing Workers on Organic Farms, Stettiner Strasse 3, W-6301 Pohlheim, Germany.

Hospitality

Arcade Hotels, Mauritiusstrasse 5–7, W–6200 Wiesbaden. Tel: 611 3 9361.

Cityhotel-Metropol, 5400 Koblenz am Rhein, Germany. Tel: 0261 350 69. Musicians wanted to play in the hotel.

Familien und Sporthotel Allgauer Berghof, 8976 Blaichach, Southern Bavaria, Germany. Tel: 08321 8060.

Ferienhaus Mittenwald, Weidenberg 1 & 3, D–8102 Mittenwald, Germany. Tel: 08823 5962/4477.

Gasthof Adler, Ehlenbogen 1, 7297 Alpirsbach Schwarzwald, Kreis Freudenstadt, Germany.

Golf-Hotel, Fremersbergstr, 113, 7570 Baden-Baden, Germany. Tel: 07221 36010.

Alpotels (Employment Agency), PO Box 388, London SW1X 8LX.

Conduct aptitude tests on behalf of German employers, for people who want to work in German hotels.

Hotel Alte Thorschenke, Bruckenstrasse 3, 5590 Cochem/Mosel, Germany. Tel: 02671 7059.

Hotel Arcade, Dachauerstrasse 21, 8000 München, Germany. Tel: 089 551930.

Hotel Bayerischer Hof, Seepromenade, 8990 Lindau, Germany.

Hotel Bold, Ringhotel Oberammergau, König-Ludwig Strasse 10, 8103 Oberammergau, Germany.

Hotel-Restaurant, Burgfrieden, J. M. Mühlental 62, 5591 Beilstein/ Mosel, Germany.

Hotel am Hochwald, Carl-Oelemann-Weg 9, 6530 Bad Nauheim, Germany. Tel: 06032 3480.

Hotel Königssee-Betriebe, Seestrasse 29, 8240 Königssee-Berchtesgaden, Upper Bavaria, Germany.

Hotel Prinz-Luitpold-Bad, 8973 Hindelang/Allgau, Bavarian Alps, Germany.

Hotel Schloss Petershagen, Schlosstrasse 5–7, 4953 Petershagen 1, Germany.

Hotel Schimmel, 8973 Hindelang, Germany. Tel: 08324 459.

Hotel Wittelsbacher Hof, 8989 Obertsdorf, Prinzenstrasse 24, Germany. Tel: 08322 605 0.

Hotel Wolf, Dorfstrasse 1, 8103 Oberammergau, Germany. Tel: 0822 3071.

Parkhotel Wehrle, Gartenstrasse 24, 7740 Triberg im Schwarzwald, Germany. Tel: 77 22 86 02 0.

Pohl's Rheinhotel Adler, 5422 St. Goarshausen-Loreleystadt, Germany. Tel: 067 71 613.

Rheinhotel Loreley, Rheinallee 12, 5330 Königswinter 1, Germany. Tel: 0 22 23 2 30 13.

Romantic Hotel 'Zur Oberen Linde', 7602 Oberkirch, Germany. Tel: 78 02 80 20.

Schlosshotel Lisl und Jägerhaus, Neuschwansteiner 1–3, 8959, Hohenschwangau, Germany.

Steigenberger Hotel Axelmannstein, Salzburger Strasse 2–6, 8230 Bad Reichenhall, Germany.

Steigenberger Inselhotel, Auf der Insel 1, 7750 Germany.

Waldhotel Forellenhof, 7570 Baden-Baden, Gaisbach 91, Germany.

Voluntary work

Community work

British Forces Germany, Chief Youth Service Officer, BFG Youth Service, Education Branch, HQ, British Army of the Rhine,

BFPO 140. Tel: 010 49 2161 472 3176. Run the Summer Student Volunteers Scheme for student teachers and young people to work with youngsters in Germany.

Camphill Schools, Heimsonderschule Brachenreuthe, W–7770 Uberlingen-Bodensee, Germany. Tel: 07551 80070. Require volunteers to work with mentally handicapped children.

Conservation

British Trust For Conservation Volunteers, Room IWH, 36 St. Mary's Street, Wallingford, Oxfordshire OX10 0EU. Run short conservation programmes near Munich.

Christlicher Friedensdienst EV, Rendelerstrasse 9–11, W–6000 Frankfurt-Bornheim. Tel: 069 459071 72. Work to create protected areas for wildlife. (Apply through Christian Movement for Peace, Bethnal Green United Reformed Church, Pott Street, London E2 0EF).

Internationale Jugendgemeinschafts Dienste EV, Kaiserstrasse 43, W–5300 Bonn 1, Germany. Run a variety of conservation and restoration programmes throughout Germany. (Apply through Concordia, 8 Brunswick Place, Hove, East Sussex BN3 1ET.)

Work camps

Internationaler Bauorden-Deutscher Zweig EV, Liebigstrasse 23 PO Box 1438, W–6520 Worms-Horchheim, Germany. Run work camps to help the underprivileged.

Nothelfergemeinschaft der Freunde EV, Secretariat General, Auf der Kornerwiese 5, W–6000 Frankfurt-am-Main 1, Germany. Run work camps to help children, the elderly and the mentally handicapped.

Pro International, Bahnhofstrasse 26 A, 3550 Marburg/L, Germany. Run work camps promoting 'Peace through Friendship'.

Other useful addresses

The Axel Springer Publishing Group, Unit 2, Princeton Court, 53/55 Felsham Road, London SW15 1BY. Tel: (081) 789 4929. Can place job advertisements in German newspapers.

Publicitas Limited, 517/523 Fulham Road, London SW6 1HD. Tel: (071) 385 7723. Can place job advertisements in German newspapers.

Youth and Student Information, Artu Berliner Gesellschaft für Studenten und Jugendaustausch GmbH, Hardenbergstrasse 9, W–1 Berlin 12, (Charlottenburg), Germany.

Temporary work rating
Good. As with other EU countries there is freedom of movement for UK citizens. However, Germany is currently experiencing one of its worst recessions of modern times and this is having two effects. First, there are fewer jobs to be had and so competition is greater. Secondly, there is a growing resentment to foreigners taking jobs that could be given to German workers. This is manifesting itself particularly in the actions of some extreme right-wing movements and it is worth keeping in mind when looking for work in Germany.

Greece

Greek Embassy, 1A Holland Park, London W11 3TP. Tel: (071) 727 8040.

Visa/work permit requirements
UK citizens do not require work permits or visas.

Length of stay permitted
You can stay in Greece for up to three months without any formality. If you want to stay longer you will have to apply for a residence permit. This is done by going to the Aliens Department of the Ministry of Public Order in Athens, or any local police station outside Athens. You should take your passport, a letter of intent of employment and a medical certificate (preferably obtained from a local hospital in Greece). Initially a six month visa will be issued after which it will be extended to five years.

Types of temporary work available
Au pair, camp couriers, fruit-picking, hospitality, labouring and voluntary work.

Official recruitment agencies
The Greek national employment service is the **Organisimos Apasholisseos Ergatikou Dynamikou (OAED)**. There are a few private employment agencies and these can usually be found under 'Grafia Apasholisis' in the *Yellow Pages*.

Prospective employers
Au pairs
Anglia Agency, 70 Southsea Avenue, Leigh-on-Sea, Essex. Tel: (0702) 471648.
Galentinas Childcare Consultancy, PO Box 51181, 145 10 Kifissia,

Greece. Tel: 1 808 1005.

Students Abroad Limited, 11 Milton View, Hitchin, Herts SG4 0QD. Tel: (0462) 438909.

Camp couriers

Best Travel Limited, 31 Topsfield Parade, Crouch End, London N8 8PT. Tel: (081) 341 7065.

Mark Warner, 20 Kensington Church Street, London W8 4EP. Tel: (071) 937 4832.

See also Chapter 4.

Fruit-picking

There is various fruit-picking work in Greece from April to October. The Peloponnesian peninsula and Crete are the most productive areas but it is definitely a case of applying to the farms in person. Competition can be quite fierce and wages are moderate but perseverance should pay off. The best place to look for work is at a town's main café, first thing in the morning.

Hospitality

Colossus Beach Hotel, PO Box 105, Faliraki, Rhodes, Greece.

Corina's Place-Il Giardino, Logaras, Paros, Greece. Tel: 01030 284 4109.

Hotel Agios Gordis, Thyris Kerkyras, Corfu, Greece.

Hotel Orpheus, 58 Haldokondili Street, Athens, Greece. Tel: 01 5224996/5237473.

Working Holidays, 11 Nikis Street, (Syntagma Square), Athens 105.57, Greece. Tel: 322 4321/325 5168.

Xenia Hotel, Mitilini, Lesbos, Greece.

Voluntary work

British Trust For Conservation Volunteers, Room IWH, 36 St Mary's Street, Wallingford, Oxfordshire OX10 0EU. A variety of conservation work throughout Greece.

European Conservation Volunteers Greece, 15 Omirou Street, 14562 Kifissia, Greece. Organise international work camps. (Apply through United Nations Association International Youth Service, Temple of Peace, Cathays Park, Cardiff CF1 3AP.)

Service Civil International, 43 Avlonos Street, 10443 Athens, Greece. Organise various projects throughout Greece. (Apply through International Voluntary Service, Old Hall, East Bergholt, Colchester, Essex CO7 6TQ.

Useful addresses

Publicitas Limited, 517/523 Fulham Road, London SW6 1HD. Tel:

(071) 385 7723. Can place job advertisements in Greek newspapers.

The Athens News, 23–25 Lekka Street 10562, Athens, Greece. Tel: 01 322 4253. Accepts job advertisements.

General Information: 11 Nikis Street, 2nd Floor, Syntagma Square, 105 57 Athens, Greece. Tel: 1 322 1267/323 3767.

Temporary work rating

Very good. Greece is probably one of the best countries on the temporary job map for people picking up casual work once they are in the country, particularly in tourism. Over 7 million tourists go to Greece each year, and there is a vast network of pubs, restaurants, hotels, tavernas and cafés to service them. Many of these businesses employ temporary workers, some of whom stay in their jobs longer than others. If you spend enough time knocking on doors in the tourist areas then it is highly likely that you will land a job sooner or later. The island resorts have proved happy hunting grounds for temporary workers in the past.

Hungary

Hungarian Embassy, 35 Eaton Place, London SW1X 8BY. Tel: (071) 235 4048.

Visa/work permit requirements

UK citizens do not need visas to travel to Hungary but if they are going to take up a job they need a work permit. This must be applied for by the employer, in Britain, before you take up your job.

Temporary work rating

Poor. As the Hungarian Embassy says, 'There is no central or local agency offering temporary jobs for foreigners. Owing to the nearly one million unemployed people in Hungary, it is almost impossible to get a temporary job'. Of course this does not mean that it is totally impossible but it should be looked upon as a challenge. Probably the best way of working in Hungary is to work for a voluntary organisation. In addition to those in Chapter 4 you could try:

Biokultura Association, 1023 Budapest, Tork st. 7 V/1, Hungary. Tel: 36 1 136 88 52. Run organic farms.

HELP (Scotland), 60 The Pleasance, Edinburgh EH8 9JT. Tel: (031) 556 9497. Sends volunteers to Hungary to help create self-sufficient communities.

International Farm Experience Programme, YFC Centre, National

Agricultural Centre, Kenilworth, Warwickshire CV8 2LG.

Iceland

Icelandic Embassy, 1 Eaton Terrace, London SW1W 8EY. Tel: (071) 730 5131.

Visa/work permit requirements
UK citizens do not require a visa to visit Iceland but a work permit is required for any type of employment. This must be obtained prior to visiting Iceland and must be applied for at the Ministry of Social Affairs by the prospective employer.

Length of stay permitted
Up to three months.

Temporary job rating
Poor. Iceland is a notoriously difficult location for temporary workers. In the past, people have found employment in the fish processing industry. While this is still a possibility it is one that seems to be on the wane. The general situation is summed up by the Icelandic Embassy: 'Our information is that there are no job opportunities for foreigners at the present time'.

Italy

Italian Embassy, 14 Three Kings Yard, London W1Y 2EH. Tel: (071) 629 8200.

Visa/work permit requirements
UK citizens do not require visas to enter Italy to look for work. However, once work has been found a work permit must be applied for. This is issued by the local authorities to the employer. But be warned: Italian bureaucracy is second to none as far as red tape is concerned and by the time you obtain the relevant papers you may have finished your job and moved on. Many people find it easier to bypass the red tape altogether.

Length of stay permitted
Three months while looking for work. Indefinite once work has been found.

Types of temporary work available
Au pair, camp couriers, fruit-picking, hospitality and voluntary work.

Official recruitment agencies

The official Italian employment office is the **Ufficio de Collocamento Manadopera.**

Prospective employers

Au pairs

Anglo Pair Agency, 40 Wavertree Road, Streatham Hill, London SW2 3SP. Tel: (081) 674 3605.

Au Pairs – Italy, 46 The Rise, Sevenoaks, Kent TN13 1RJ. Tel: (0732) 451 522.

Helping Hands Au Pair and Domestic Agency, 39 Rutland Avenue, Thorpe Bay, Essex SS1 2XJ. Tel: (0702) 602067.

Home From Home, Walnut Orchard, Chearsley, Aylesbury, Buckinghamshire HP18 0DA.

Universal Care, Chester House, 9 Windsor End, Beaconsfield, Buckinghamshire HP9 2JJ.

Camp couriers

See Chapter 4.

Fruit-picking

Italy has a fruit-picking season that stretches from May to December. The majority of produce is located in the north of the country. You can try applying at a local office of the national employment service but you might be more successful befriending a local farmer.

Hospitality

Albergo Ristorante Colibri, Via Cristoforo Colombo 57, 17024 Finale Ligure (Savona), Italy.

Bladon Lines, 56–58 Putney High Street, London SW15 2SF. Tel: (081) 785 2200. Employ chalet staff in Italy.

Crystal Holdiays, Crystal House, The Courtyard, Arlington Road, Surbiton, Surrey KT6 6BW. Tel: (081) 390 8737. Employ chalet staff in the Italian Alps.

Eurotel Garda, Via Marconi 18, 37016 Garda, Italy.

Hotel Cannero, 28051 Cannero Riviera, Lake Maggiore, Italy. Tel: 323 788046.

Hotel Cavallino d'Oro, 39040 Castelrotto (BZ), Sudtirol, Dolomites, Italy.

Hotel Pensione La Lanterna, Via Osteria, 53030 Livigno (50), Italy.

Hotel Villa Condulmer, Via Zermanese 1, 31021 Mogliano Veneto, Italy.

Voluntary work

Alternative Travel Group Limited, Restoration Project, 69–71 Banbury Road, Oxford OX2 6PE. Tel: (0865) 310399. Volunteers required to help with the restoration of a convent in Tuscany.

Associazione Italiana Costruttori, Via Cesare Battisti 3, 20071 Casalpusterlengo (MI), Italy. Run work camps to help all disadvantaged sections of society.

Comunita Emmaus, Segretariato Campi dei Lavoro, Via la Luna 1, 52020 Pergine Valdarno (AR), Italy. Run work camps throughout Italy.

Gruppi Archeologici d'Italia, Via Tacito 41, 00193 Rome, Italy. Tel: 06 6874028. Volunteers required to work on archaeological digs in Italy.

Other useful addresses

Publicitas Limited, 517/523 Fulham Road, London SW6 1HD. Tel: (071) 385 7723. Can place job advertisements in Italian newpapers.

Smyth International, 23a Aylmer Parade, London N2 0PQ. Can place job advertisements in Italian newspapers.

Temporary work rating

Good. There is a variety of temporary work to be found in Italy. The one big drawback is the hassle you have to go through trying to get the correct paperwork from the authorities. In many cases it is possible to work unofficially and employers are quite often happy to do this because they are as irritated by officialdom as everyone else.

Luxembourg

Luxembourg Embassy, 27 Wilton Crescent, London SW1X. Tel: (071) 235 6961.

Visa/work permit requirements

UK citizens do not require a visa to enter Luxembourg to look for work. Once a job has been found you must apply for an identity card, which serves as a residence permit. This is done by taking your passport, proof of sufficient means of subsistence, a medical certificate issued by a Luxembourg doctor, a certificate of proof of residence in Luxembourg and, if possible, a character reference, to the **Police des Etrangers**, Ministère de la Justice, 16 boulevard Royal, Luxembourg. Tel: 4794 450.

Length of stay permitted

Three months while looking for work. Indefinite once work has been found.

Types of temporary work available

Principally hospitality but there are some openings for camp couriers and au pairs.

Official recruitment agencies

There are a number of national employment agencies in Luxembourg, some of which deal specifically with temporary jobs:

Administration de l'Emploi, 38a rue Philippe II, Luxembourg. Tel: 47 68 55 1 (general Labour Exchange).

Manpower-Aide Temporaire, Sarl, 19 rue Glesener, Luxembourg. Tel: 48 23 23 (agency for temporary jobs).

Bureau-Service, Sarl, 2 allée Leopold Goebel, Luxembourg. Tel: 44 45 04/44/45 62 93 (temporary office jobs).

Service National de la Jeunesse, 1 rue de la Poste, Luxembourg. Tel: 46 80 2 331 (Department of the Minister of Education — dealing with student employment).

Officenter, 25 bld Royal, Luxembourg. Tel: 47 25 62 (temporary office jobs for students).

Adia, Luxembourg Sarl, 70 Grand rue, L 1660 Luxembourg. Tel: 46 08 68 (temporary jobs for students).

Prospective employers

Hospitality

Hôtel Air-Field, 6 route de Trèves (2632), Luxembourg. Tel: 43 19 34.

Hôtel Alfa, 16 place de la Gare, BP 2033 (1020), Luxembourg. Tel: 49 00 11.

Hôtel Arcotel, 43 avenue de la Gare (1611), Luxembourg. Tel: 49 40 01.

Hôtel des Ardennes, 59 avenue de la Liberté, Luxembourg. Tel: 48 81 41.

Hôtel Axe, 32–34 rue Joseph Junck (1839), Luxembourg. Tel: 49 09 53.

Hôtel Central Molitor, 28 avenue de la Liberté (1930), Luxembourg. Tel: 48 99 11.

Hôtel Dauphin, 42 avenue de la Gare, Luxembourg. Tel: 48 82 82.

Hôtel Euro, 114 route d'Arlon, (1150), Luxembourg. Tel: 44 65 37.

Hôtel Inter-Continental, 12 rue Jean Engling, BP 1313 (1013), Luxembourg. Tel 4 37 81.

Hôtel Italia, 15–17 rue d'Anvers (1130), Luxembourg. Tel: 48 66 26.

Hôtel Marco Polo, 27 rue du Fort Neipperg (2230), Luxembourg. Tel: 40 64 14-1.
Hôtel Le Parisien, 46 rue Zithe (2763), Luxembourg. Tel: 49 23 97.
Hôtel Président, 32 place de la Gare, BP (2480), Luxembourg. Tel: 48 61 61.
Hôtel Le Royal, 12 boulevard Royal (2449), Luxembourg. Tel: 4 16 16.
Hôtel Sheraton Aérogolf, route de Trèves-Findel BP 1973 (1019), Luxembourg. Tel: 3 45 71.
Hôtel Zurich, 36 rue Joseph Junck (1839), Luxembourg. Tel: 49 13 50.
Hôtel Diligence, 17 rue du Lac (8808), Arsdorf. Tel: 6 42 63.
Hôtel Ecu de Beaufort, 11 rue de l'Eglise (6315), Beaufort. Tel 8 61 18.
Hôtel Central Cabana, 9 place Princesse Maria Theresa (9710), Clervaux. Tel: 9 11 05.
Hôtel Au Bon Accueil, 75–79 avenue de la Gare (9233), Diekirch. Tel: 80 34 76.
Hôtel du Commerce, 16 place du Marché (6460), Echernach. Tel: 7 23 01.
Hôtel de la Poste, 107 rue de l'Alzette (4010), Esh-Sur-Alzette. Tel: 5 35 04.
Hôtel Dolce Vita, 4 avenue Dr. Klein (5630), Mondorf-les-Bains. Tel: 6 80 73.
Hôtel des Ardennes, 29 rue de la Gare (55400), Remich. Tel: 69 94 31.
Hôtel Nagel, 2 rue de Bettel BP 43 (9401), Vianden. Tel: 8 45 05.
Hôtel de Vianden, 1 route de Diekirch (9409), Vianden. Tel: 8 40 01.

Other useful addresses

Letzeburger Journal, rue A Fischer 123, PO Box 2101, Luxembourg and *Luxemburger Wort*, rue Christophe-Plantin 2, 2988 Gasperich-Luxembourg are two national newspapers that carry job advertisements.
Luxembourg-Accueil Informations, 10 Bisserwee, L–1238 Luxembourg. Tel: 4 17 17. Can help arrange au pair positions.
Institut Viti-Vinicole, Boîte Postale 50 (5501) Remich. Tel: 6 91 22. Can help with information regarding the grape harvest.

Temporary work rating

Good, but it is worth considering that Luxembourg is a very small country (total population 385,000, 75,500 of which live in Luxembourg city) and so work opportunities are naturally fewer than in larger countries. However, foreign workers are encouraged to take up employment in Luxembourg (Luxembourg has the highest proportion of foreigners of any EU country) and temporary job seekers are given a warm welcome and a considerable amount of help. One point to remember is that both French and German are spoken in Luxembourg and so you should have some knowledge of at least one of these languages if you hope to work in this country.

Malta

Maltese High Commission, 16 Kensington Square, London W8 5HH. Tel: (071) 938 1712.

Visa/work permit requirements

UK citizens require work permits to take up any employment in Malta. Work permits must be applied for by the prospective employer on behalf of the foreign employee. The employer must also show sufficient proof that the foreign worker will fill a position for which no skilled Maltese national is available.

Types of temporary work available

Very limited. There is a thriving tourist industry in Malta and therefore there will be openings in the hospitality industry — although this may have to be done by by-passing the formidable restrictions on work permits.

Useful addresses

Malta Youth Hostel Association, 17 Triq Tal-Borg, Pawla PLA 06, Malta. Tel: 356 693957. Volunteers can work in youth hostels in Malta and in return for a 21 hour week they receive free accommodation. A work permit is required for this.

British Universities North America Club (BUNAC), 16 Bowling Green Lane, London EC1R 0BD. Tel: (071) 251 3472. Run a Work Malta programme for catering students who wish to gain experience in the catering business abroad.

Temporary work rating

Moderate. If you follow the official line you will deduce that finding a temporary job in Malta is virtually impossible. However, for the freelance operator there are openings in hotels, pubs and restaurants.

Netherlands

Royal Netherlands Embassy, 38 Hyde Park Gate, London SW7 5DP. Tel: (071) 584 5040.

Visa/work permit requirements

UK citizens do not need visas to enter the Netherlands. Anyone who intends to work must register within eight days with the Police Immigration Department (Vreemdelingenpolitie). If you intend to work for more than three months you need to apply for a residence permit (verblijfsvergunning).

Length of stay permitted

Three months while looking for work. Indefinite once work has been found.

Types of temporary work available

Agricultural work, au pair, factory work, hospitality, office work and voluntary work.

Official recruitment agencies

The official Dutch employment service is the **Central Bureau voor de Arbeidsvoorziening**. To obtain a list of their regional offices write to their head offices at, Videoing 26, Postbus 5814, 2280 HV Rijswijk (2-H). Tel: 070 3130911.

The Dutch equivalent of British Jobcentres is the **Arbeidsbureau (AB)**. There are offices all over the country and these can be found in the Dutch equivalent of the *Yellow Pages*, *Gouden Gids*.

Private agencies (**Uitzendbureaux**) can also be found in the *Gouden Gids.*

There are a number of organisations who specialise in temporary employment:

Project Bureau 'Bolwerk', Dorpen 22, 1741 EE Schagen, The Netherlands. Tel: 02242 17057. Provides written material on temporary employment.

Central Office of the Employment Service, Bureau IABS (International Placement and Trainee Schemes), PO Box 437, 2280 AK Rijswijk, The Netherlands. Tel: 070 3130228. Process applications for temporary employment of at least 6 weeks.

Prospective employers

Au pairs

Academy Au Pair Agency, Glenlea, Dulwich Common, London SE21 7ES. Tel: (081) 299 4599.

Avalon Agency, Thursley House, 53 Station Road, Shalford, Guildford, Surrey GU4 8HA Tel: (0483) 63640.

Langtrain International, Torquay Road, Foxrock, Dublin 18,

Ireland. Tel: 1 289 3876.
Students Abroad Limited, 11 Milton View, Hitchin, Herts, SG4 0QD. Tel: (0462) 438909.

Factory work

Algemene Studenten Arbeidsverlening, Rapenburg 91, 2311 GK Leiden, The Netherlands. Employ several hundred temporary staff to work on the production line.

Farm work

Centraal Bureau Arbeidsvoorziening, Bureau Internationale Arbeidsbemiddeling en Stagiaires, PO Box 437, 2280 AK Rijswijk, The Netherlands.
International Farm Experience Programme, YFC Centre, National Agricultural Centre, Stoneleigh Park, Kenilworth, Warwickshire CV8 2LG. Tel: (0203) 696584.

Horticulture

The bulb industry is one of the major ones as far as the temporary worker is concerned and there is usually a shortage of workers at the height of the season, from June to October. Many company and family-owned farms employ workers during this period:
Baartman and Koning BV, PO Box 27–2170 AA Sassenheim, Teylingerlaan 7, 2215 RT Voorhout, The Netherlands. Tel: 02522 11141.
Walter Blom, Hyacinthenlaan 2, 2182 DE Hillegom, The Netherlands. Tel: 02520 19444.
Noorder Leidsvaart 26, 2182 NB Hillegom, The Netherlands. Tel: 02520 16608.
Unex, Heereweg 17B, 2161 AC Lisse, The Netherlands, Tel: 02521 11342.

Hospitality

Hotel Apple Inn, Koninginne Weg 93, 1075 CJ Amsterdam, The Netherlands.
Motel-Café-Restaurant De Witte Bergen, Rijksweg 2, Eemnes, The Netherlands. Tel: 02153 86754.
Hotel Opduin, De Koog, Texel, The Netherlands.
Hotel Wilhemina/Hotel King, 167–169 Koninginne Weg 167–169, 1075 CN Amsterdam, The Netherlands.

Voluntary work

Most voluntary positions in The Netherlands are dealt with by related organisations in the UK.

Other useful addreses

The Federation of Recruitment and Employment Services Limited (FRES), 36–38 Mortimer Street, London W1N 7RB. Tel: (071) 323 4300. Can provide the names of private employment agencies in the UK who can place employees in the Netherlands.

Powers Overseas Limited, Duncan House, Dolphin Square, London SW1V 3PS. Tel: (071) 834 5566. Can place job advertisements in newspapers in The Netherlands.

De Telegraaf, Basisweg 30, 1043 AP Amsterdam, The Netherlands. Tel: 010 20 585 9111. A major newspaper in The Netherlands that carries job advertisements.

Temporary work rating

Very good. The Netherlands offers a variety of temporary work opportunities. Their speciality is in the horticulture industry and as long as you do not mind undertaking repetitive work then there should be an opening here at some time in the growing season.

Norway

Royal Norwegian Embassy, 25 Belgrave Square, London SW1X 8QD. Tel: (071) 235 7151.

Visa/work permit requirements

UK citizens do not need visas or work permits to work in Norway. Although the Norwegian authorities like to keep a close eye on workers in their country there is a moderate amount of work to be found.

Length of stay permitted

Three months, after which you need to apply for a residence permit.

Types of temporary work available

Limited, but there are openings in farm work, hospitality and voluntary work. There are also limited openings for au pairs and camp couriers.

Official recruitment agencies

The official employment service in Norway is **arbeidsformidlingen, arbeidskontoret.**

Prospective employers

Au pairs

Atlantis Youth Exchange, Rolf Hofmosgate 18, 0655 Oslo 6,

Norway. They can arrange for a small number of au pairs to work for Norwegian families. The same organisation also arranges for young people to stay on farms in Norway as working guests.

Camp couriers

Eurocamp, Summer Jobs, PO Box 170, Liverpool L70 1ES.

Hospitality

Elveseter Hotel, 2687 Elveseter, Norway.
Hovringen Hogfjellshotel, 2679 Hovringen, Norway.
Kvikne's Hotel, 5850 Balestrand, Norway.
Lindstrom Hotel, 5890 Lardal, Norway. Tel: 056 66202.
Sandven Hotel, PO Box 160, 5600 Norheimsund, Norway.
Stalheim Hotel, 5715 Stalheim, Norway.
Hotel Ullensvang, 5774 Lofthus, Hardanger, Norway.
Hotel Voringfoss, 5783 Eidfjord i Hardanger, Norway.

Voluntary work

International Farm Experience Programme, YFC Centre, National Agricultural Centre, Stoneleigh Park, Kenilworth, Warwickshire CV8 2LG. Tel: (0203) 696584.

Nansen International Children's Center, Barnegarden Breivold, Nessest, 1433 Vinterbro, Norway. Require volunteers to work at a relief centre for troubled teenagers.

Other voluntary work can be sought through the relevant organisations in the UK who operate in Norway.

Other useful addresses

Frank L. Crane Limited, 5/15 Cromer Street, Gray's Inn Road, London WC1H 8LS. Tel: (071) 837 3330. Can place job advertisements in Norwegian newspapers.

Power Overseas Limited, 46 Keyes House, Dolphin Square, London SW1V 3NA. Can place job advertisements in Norwegian newspapers.

Temporary work rating

Moderate. Work can be found in hotels and restaurants and also at ski resorts around the country. There is also a possibility of working in factories or on farms.

Poland

Polish Embassy, 47 Portland Place, London W1N 3AG. Tel: (071) 580 4324.

Visa/work permit requirements
UK citizens do not need a visa to visit Poland.

Length of stay permitted
Up to 6 months.

Types of temporary work available
Very limited. Almost all of the opportunities are through voluntary organisations:

Anglo-Polish Academic Association, Secretariat, 93 Victoria Road, Leeds LS6 1DR. Tel: (0532) 758121. Require volunteers to teach English to Polish doctors, teachers and students.

Brit-Pol Health Care Foundation, Gerrard House, Suite 14, Worthing Road, East Preston, West Sussex BN16 1AW. Tel: (0903) 859222. Require a small number of teachers to work on summer camps for children.

Foundation for International Youth Exchanges. Ul Grzybowska 79, 00-844 Warsaw, Poland. Run work camps for disadvantaged groups.

Agricultural Centre, Stoneleigh Park, Kenilworth, Warwickshire CV8 2LG. Tel: (0203) 696584.

Temporary work rating
Very poor, particularly for the freelance job seeker.

Portugal

Portuguese Embassy, 11 Belgrave Square, London SW1X 8PP. Tel: (071) 581 8722.

Visa/work permit requirements
UK citizens do not require a visa or a work permit to work in Portugal. However, a residence permit is required if you intend to work in Portugal for more than 3 months. This will be issued from the nearest office of the Foreigner's Department of the Ministry of Internal Affairs (**Servico de Estrangeiros**) on production of confirmation of your employment.

Length of stay permitted
Up to 3 months while looking for work. Indefinite once a job has been found.

Types of temporary work available
Au pair, camp couriers, hospitality and voluntary work.

Official recruitment agencies

The Portuguese equivalent of UK Jobcentres is the **Centro doe Emprego** which is run by the **Ministerio de Emprego e Seguranca Social**. It can be used freely by UK citizens.

Some prospective employers

Au pairs

Centro de Intercambio e Turismo Universitario, avenida Defensores de Chaves, 67–6, Dto, Lisbon, Portugal.

Turicoop, rua Pascoal de Melo, 15–1, Dto, 1100 Lisbon, Portugal.

Camp couriers

Seasun/Tentrek Holidays, 71/72 East Hill, Colchester, Essex CO1 2QW. Tel: (0206) 861886.

Voluntary work

Associacao de Turismo Estudentil e Juvenil, rua Joaquim Antonio Aguiar No. 255, 4300 Oporto, Portugal. Tel: 568542. Require volunteers to work on projects throughout Portugal.

Companheiros Construtores, rua Pedro Monteiro 3–1, Coimbra, Portugal. Tel: 039 716747. Require volunteers to work helping underprivileged communities throughout Portugal.

Fundo de Apoio aos Organizmos Juvenis, rua Duque de Avila 137, 1097 Lisbon, Portugal. Tel: 535081. Require a large number of volunteers to work on a vareity of projects throughout Portugal.

Other useful addresses

Publicitas Limited, 517-523 Fulham Road, London SW6 1HD. Tel: (071) 385 7723. Can place job advertisements in Portuguese newspapers.

Anglo-Portuguese News, Apartado 113, 2765 Estoril, Lisbon, Portugal. An English language newspaper which publishes all types of job advertisements.

Federation of Recruitment and Employment Services Limited, 36–38 Mortimer Street, London W1N 7RB. They have a list of UK agencies who deal with work abroad.

Temporary work rating

Average. Since EU nationals do not require work permits for Portugal there are some employment possibilities, but not as many as in neighbouring Spain. There is work to be found in the tourist industry, although fruit-picking remains a hard nut to crack.

Romania

Romanian Embassy, 4 Palace Green, London W8 4QD. Tel: (071) 937 9666.

Visa/work permit requirements

UK citizens require a visa to visit Romania.

Length of stay permitted

Varies.

Types of temporary work available

Very limited — the opportunities for employment rest almost exclusively with voluntary organisations.

Useful addresses

British Trust For Conservation Volunteers, Room IWH, 36 St. Mary's Street, Wallingford, Oxfordshire OX10 0EU. Require volunteers for practical conservation work in Romania.

Crystal Holidays, Crystal House, The Courtyard, Arlington Road, Surbiton, Surrey KT6 6BW. Tel: (081) 390 8737. Require representatives for their skiing holidays in Romania.

A number of British based charities require volunteers to work in Romania (see Chapter 4).

Temporary work rating

Very poor. There is little chance of travelling to Romania and finding paid temporary work. The most likely option is to obtain a place with a volunteer organisation.

Spain

Spanish Embassy, 24 Belgrave Square, London SW1X 8QA. Tel: (071) 235 5555.

Visa/work permit requirements

UK citizens do not require a visa to enter Spain. If you intend to stay for more than 3 months you will require a residence card (**Tarjeta Comunitaria Europea**). These can be obtained from either the Foreign Nationals Office (**Oficina de Extranjeria**) or the nearest county central police station (**Comisaria Provincial de Policia**). You will need to produce a valid passport and a photocopy of the same, three passport-sized photographs, a medical certificate and a contract or offer of employment.

Length of stay permitted

Indefinite once a residence card has been issued, although it will probably need to be renewed after a year and then 5 years after that.

Types of temporary work available

Au pair, camp courier, hospitality, teaching English and voluntary work.

Official recruitment agencies

The official Spanish employment is the **Oficinas de Empleo**, offices of which can be found all over Spain.

Prospective employers

Au pairs

About Au Pairs, 3 Garston Park, Godstone, Surrey RH9 8NE. Tel: (0883) 743735.

Academy Au Pair Agency Limited, Glenlea, Dulwich Common, London SE21 7ES. Tel: (081) 299 4599.

Anglia Agency, 70 Southsea Avenue, Leigh-on-Sea, Essex. Tel: (0702) 471648.

Centros Europeos, C/principe 12, 6A, 28012 Madrid, Spain.

Club de Relaçiones Culturales Internaçionales, Calle de Ferraz 82, 28008 Madrid, Spain. Tel: 1 541 7103.

Home From Home, Walnut Orchard, Chearsley, Aylesbury, Buckinghamshire HP18 0DA. Tel: (0844) 208561.

Jolaine Agency, 18 Escot Way, Barnet, Herts EN5 3AN. Tel: (081) 449 1334.

Just The Job Employment Agency, 8 Musters Road, West Bridgford, Nottingham NG2 7JA. Tel: (0602) 813224.

Langtrain International, Torquay Road, Foxrock, Dublin 18, Ireland. Tel: 1 289 3876.

Problems Unlimited Agency, 86 Alexandra Road, Windsor, Berkshire SL4 1HU. Tel: (0753) 830101.

Students Abroad Limited, 11 Milton View, Hitchin, Herts SG4 0QD. Tel: (0462) 438909.

Universal Care, Chester House, 9 Windsor End, Beaconsfield, Buckinghamshire HP9 2JJ. Tel: (0494) 678811.

Camp couriers

Acorn Venture, 137 Worcester Road, Hagley, Stourbridge, West Midlands DY9 0NW. Tel: (0562) 882151.

Ibiza Club, Apartado Correos 73, Es Cana/Santa Eulalia del Rio, Ibiza, Balearic Islands, Spain. Tel: 971 33 06 50/51.

New Century Holidays Limited, Century House, Unit 15, Kernick Industrial Estate, Penryn, Cornwall TR10 9EP. Tel: (0326) 375959.

See also Chapter 4.

Hospitality

Carretera de Saniander, Monzou de Campos, Palencia, Spain.

Hotel Ancora, Lloret de Mar, Costa Brava, Spain.

Hotel Costa Bona, Calella de la Costa (Barcelona), Spain.

Hotel Garbi, Paseo de las Rosas, Calella de la Costa (Barcelona), Spain.

Hotel Iturrimurri, Ctra Nacional 232, 26200 Haro (la Rioja) Spain.

Hotel Monte Carlo, Lloret de Mar (Costa Brava), Spain.

Hotel Montemar, Calle Puntaires 20, Pineda de Mar (Barcelona), Spain.

Nico-Hotel-FO, CN–11, Km 150, 42240 Medinaceli (Soria), Spain. Tel: 975 326111/32603.

Hotel Rigat, Playa de Fanals, Lloret de Mar, Costa Brava, Spain.

Teaching English

Spain is one country where it is possible, and sometimes even advisable, to find short-term work as a teacher of English. This is dealt with in greater depth in Chapter 4 but there are some organisations which deal specifically with teaching English in Spain:

Berlitz Language Centre, Gran Via, 80–4, 28013 Madrid, Spain. Tel: 542586. Employ EFL teachers from October to June.

Centro de Idiomas Liverpool, Calle Libreros 11, 1, 28801 Alcalá de Henares, Madrid, Spain. Tel: 881 3184. Teachers required for a language school near Madrid.

Centros Europeos, English For Executives, C/Principe 12, 6 A, 28012 Madrid, Spain.

The Mangold Institute, Avda Marqués de Sotelo 5, Pasaje Rex, Valencia 46002, Spain. Tel: 6 352 7714/351 4556.

The Spanish Institute, 102 Eaton Square, London SW1W 9AN. Provides a list of language schools in Spain who employ teachers of English.

Voluntary work

There are various voluntary organisations working in Spain but in general these should be approached through their partner organisations in the UK (see Chapter 4).

Other useful addresses

Publicitas Limited, 517/523 Fulham Road, London SW6 1HD. Tel: (071) 385 7723. Can place job advertisements in Spanish newspapers.

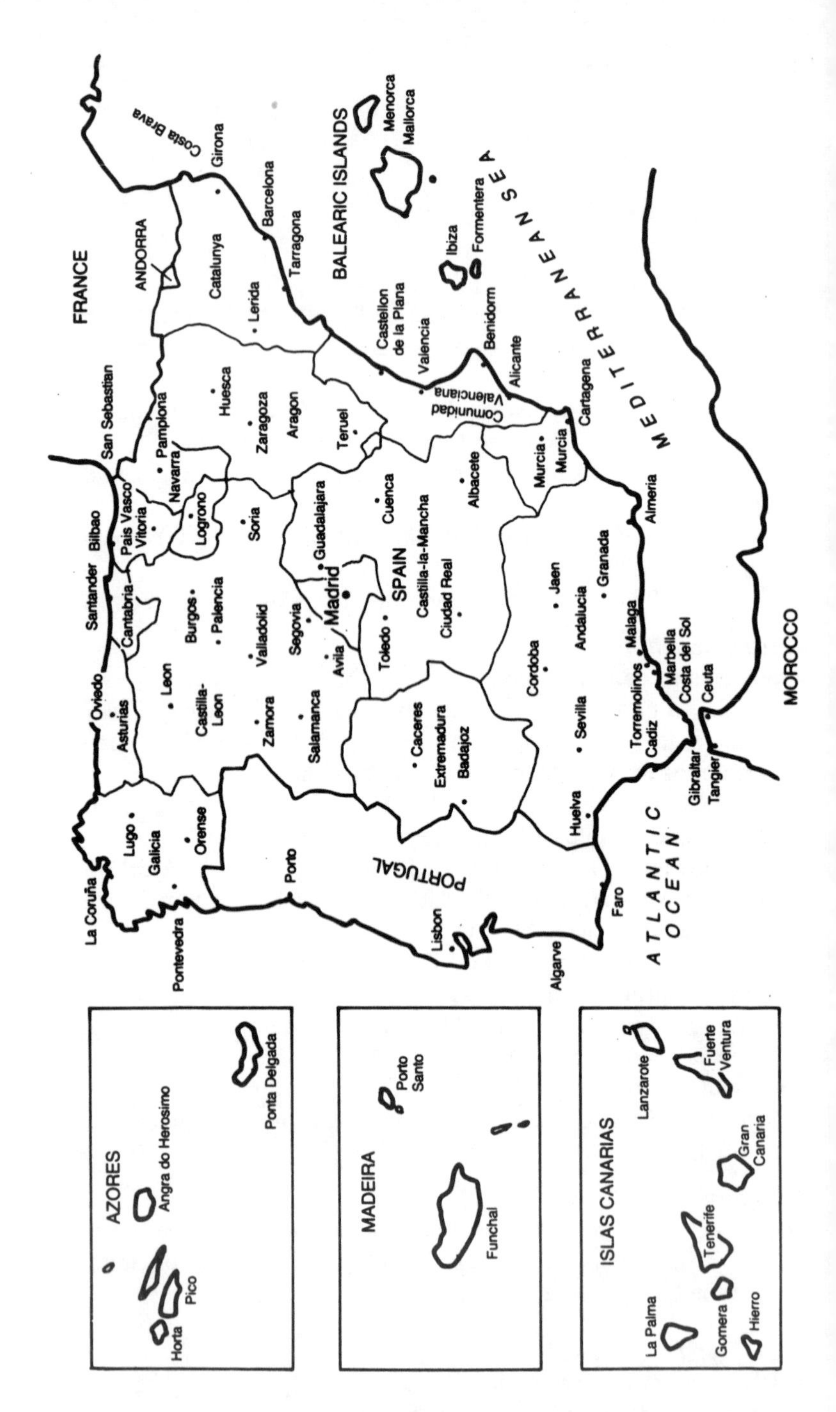

Fig. 5. Map of Spain, Portugal, the Balearic Islands, Canaries, Azores and Madeira.

Temporary work rating
Good. Due to its massive tourist industry there are numerous opportunities for temporary workers. Since the necessity for work permits has been lifted it has made it easier for UK citizens to work legally in Spain. One word of warning though — although there are a lot of jobs on offer some employers are more scrupulous than others. This can apply particularly in areas of teaching English and hospitality.

Sweden

Swedish Embassy, 11 Montagu Place, London W1H 2AL. Tel: (071) 724 2101.

Visa/work permit requirement
UK citizens do not require a visa to enter Sweden. However, a work permit is required for all types of employment. Applications should be made to the Swedish Embassy. Work permits are issued once a specific job has been found and a residence permit is required if you plan to stay for more than 3 months.

Length of stay permitted
Up to three months without a residence permit.

Types of temporary work available
Camp couriers, farm work, hospitality and voluntary work.

Official recruitment agencies
The official Swedish recruitment agency is **Arbetsmarknadsstyrelen**. They have a limited number of jobs and there are no private employment agencies that would be of any use to the temporary job seeker.

Prospective employers
Camp couriers
Eurocamp, PO Box 170, Liverpool L70 1ES.

Farm work
International Farm Experience Programme, YFC Centre, National Agriculture Centre, Stoneleigh Park, Kenilworth, Warwickshire CV8 2LG. Tel: (0203) 696584.

Voluntary work
There are various voluntary organisations working in Sweden but in

general these should be approached through their partner organisations in the UK (see Chapter 4).

Other useful addresses

Frank L. Crane (London) Limited, 5/15 Cromer Street, Gray's Inn Road, London WC1H 8LS. Tel: (071) 837 330. Can place job advertisements in Swedish newspapers.

Powers Overseas Limited, Duncan House, Dolphin Square, London SW1V 3PS. Can place job advertisements in Swedish newspapers.

Temporary work rating

Moderate. Sweden has traditionally been a tough nut to crack as far as temporary employment is concerned and since the European Economic Space has not yet been implemented the situation is unlikely to ease in the immediate future. There are temporary jobs available but the problem is obtaining a work permit. For the freelance operator there are openings in the hospitality industry and fruit-picking.

Switzerland

Swiss Embassy, 16–18 Montagu Place, London W1H 2AL. Tel: (071) 723 0701.

Visa/work permit requirements

UK citizens do not require visas to enter Switzerland but there are strict regulations governing work permits and temporary employment. There are various different work permits, the most relevant to temporary work is the seasonal permit (A Permit). This is for seasonal work in the building and hospitality industries and can be obtained after arrival in Switzerland, but only if you have an assurance of a residence permit. This in turn can only be obtained once you have the offer of a job from a Swiss employer. This is very much a case of organising work before you set off.

Length of stay permitted

Maximum 9 months on a seasonal permit.

Types of temporary work available

Au pair, camp couriers, hospitality and voluntary work.

Prospective employers

Au pairs (Au pairs also require work permits).

Helping Hands Au Pair and Domestic Agency, 39 Rutland Avenue, Thorpe Bay, Essex SS1 2XJ. Tel: (0702) 602067.

Langtrain International, Torquay Road, Foxrock, Dublin 18, Ireland. Tel: 1 289 3876.

Universal Care, Chester House, 9 Windsor End, Beaconsfield, Buckinghamshire HP9 2JJ. Tel: (0494) 678811.

Camp couriers

Lotus Travel, Alpine Operations Department, Mobbs Court, 2 Jacob Street, London SE1 2BT. Tel: (071) 962 9933. Require couriers to look after people on skiing holidays.

Venture Abroad, Warren House, High Street, Cranleigh, Surrey GU6 8AJ. Tel: (0483) 273027. Representative required to assist with holidays for youth groups.

Hospitality

Hotel Bellevue, 6440 Brunnen, Switzerland Tel: 043 31 13 18.

Hotel Belvedere, Grindelwald, Bernese Oberland, 3818, Switzerland.

Hotel Bernina Samedan, 7503 Samedan, Switzerland. Tel: 082 6 54 21.

Hotel Eden-Nova, 3800 Interlaken, Switzerland.

Hotel Freienhof, 6362 Stansstad am Vierwaldestrattersee, Switzerland.

Hotel Jungfraublick und Beauregard, Haupstrasse, CH 3803 Beatenberg, Switzerland.

Hotel Motel Krone, 3074 Berne-Muri, Switzerland.

Hotel Mond, Dorfstrasse 1, 6375 Beckenried, Switzerland.

Hotel Tellsplatte, 6452 Sisikon, near Luzern, Switzerland.

Jobs In The Alps (Employment Agency), PO Box 388, London SW1X 8LX. Recruit up to 200 staff to work in mountain resorts.

Mototel Postillon 6374 Buochs, Switzerland.

Residence and Bernerhof Hotels, 3823 Wenden, Switzerland.

Schweizer Hotelier-Verein, Monbijoustrasse 130, Postfach, 3001 Berne, Switzerland.

Voluntary work

ATD Quart Monde, 1733 Treyvaux, Switzerland. Help disadvantaged families throughout Switzerland.

Genossenschaft Camp Corti, Wasserwerkstr. 17, 8006 Zurich, Switzerland. Volunteers required for the reconstruction of an old settlement in the Alps.

Gruppo Voluntari Dalla Svizzera Italiana, CP 12, 6517 Arbedo, Switzerland. Run work camps to help mountain communities.

Internationale Begegnung In Gemeinschaftsdien-Stein eV, Schossstrasse 28, 7000 Stuttgart 1, Germany. Run work camps in

Switzerland.

Willing Workers On Organic Farms, Speerstrasse 7, 8305 Dietlikon, Switzerland. Tel: 01 834 02 34. Require volunteers to help organic farmers.

Other useful addresses

Publicitas Limited, 517/523 Fulham Road, London SW6 1HD. Tel: (071) 385 7723. Can place job advertisements in Swiss newspapers.

Temporary work rating

Moderate. If you are prepared to do the groundwork and line up a job before you go to Switzerland then you will find that there is work available. Once all the paperwork has been completed it will be a relatively efficient operation. However, people should not travel to Switzerland hoping to pick up casual work on arrival.

Turkey

Turkish Embassy, 43 Belgrave Square, London SW1X 8AP. Tel: (071) 235 5252.

Visa/work permit requirements

UK citizens do not require a visa but anyone wishing to take up employment must have a work permit. This can only be applied for once a job has been organised. An application should then be made to the Turkish Consulate General.

Length of stay permitted

Varies.

Type of temporary work available

Au pair, camp courier and voluntary work.

Official recruitment agencies

The official Turkish recruitment agency is **is ve isci Bulma Kurumu Genel Mudurlugu, 06410 Ankara, Turkey**.

Prospective employers

Au pairs

Anglo Pair Agency, 40 Wavertree Road, Streatham Hill, London SW2 3SP. Tel: (081) 674 3605.

Camp couriers

Simply Travel Limited, 8 Chiswick Terrace, Acton Lane, London W4 5LY. Tel: (081) 995 3883.

Mark Warner, 20 Kensington Church Street, London W8 4EP. Tel: (071) 937 4832.

Voluntary work

Most voluntary groups in Turkey recruit through their partner organisation in the UK (see Chapter 4).

Temporary work rating

Poor. Although it is possible to work in Turkey the most common method is through an official organisation. The work permit regulations make it very difficult for the freelance worker to find temporary work legally.

AUSTRALASIA

Australia

Consulates in the UK

South Wales and southern England

Australian High Commission, Australia House, Strand, London WC2B 4LA.

Midlands, north Wales and northern England

Australian Consulate, Chatsworth House, Lever Street, Manchester M1 2D1.

Scotland, Northern Ireland, Northumberland and Tyne & Wear

Australian Consulate, 2nd Floor, Hobart House, 80 Hanover Street, Edinburgh EH2 2DL.

Apart from the 10,000 miles that separate it from the UK Australia is in many respects the mecca for the temporary job seeker: it has a visa designed specifically for the purpose and, despite a severe recession during the last five years, there are enough employment openings to keep even the most critical worker happy for several months. It is true that it is not as easy as it once was to find temporary work in Australia and some people have found it very difficult. But if you accept that you will have to do a bit more than just tumble off the plane at Sydney then you should be able to find some form of employment Down Under.

Visa requirements

Holiday working visas

These are available to single people, or childless couples, between the ages of 18 and 25. In some exceptional cases people of up to 30 years will be considered.

The main idea behind holiday working visas is to provide young people with a chance to see Australia and supplement their travels with periods of casual employment. There are nine main conditions which applicants must fulfil:

1. The prime purpose of the visit is a temporary stay in Australia and permanent settlement is not intended.

2. Employment is incidental to the holiday and is to be used as a supplement to the money you bring with you.

3. Employment in Australia must not be pre-arranged except on a private basis and on the applicant's own initiative.

4. There must be a reasonable prospect of the applicant obtaining temporary employment to supplement holiday funds.

5. Applicants must show that they have reasonable funds to support themselves for some of their time in Australia, and return air fare. This is approximately £2,000 for one year.

6. Applicants must meet normal character requirements, and health standards where necessary.

7. Full-time employment should not be undertaken for more than three months with one employer.

8. Applicants must leave Australia after their holiday working visa has expired.

9. The maximum length of stay is twelve months.

Applications can be sent to any Australian Consulate in Britain and with them you will need to include:

- Three recent passport-sized photographs of yourself, which should be signed on the back.

- Evidence of funds for the duration of your stay plus your return air fare. If you do not think you have enough money at the time of application it is a good idea to borrow some money, pay it into a bank or building society account, obtain a statement and then repay the money. However, it is unwise to arrive in Australia without sufficient funds. Immigration officers may not investigate your financial situation when you arrive in the country but if they do they will want to see that you have access to a substantial sum of money.

- A valid passport. This should be valid for at least three months *after* your proposed departure date from Australia. If your passport does not comply with this it will be necessary to get a new one.

- A stamped self-addressed envelope for the return of your passport.

You should not apply for a holiday working visa more than four weeks before your proposed departure date. Application forms should be filled in carefully as incomplete ones will be returned unprocessed. It is not advisable to telephone to see how your application is progressing. This will only irritate Consulate staff and it will not hasten the arrival of your visa. People holding UK, Irish, Canadian, Dutch or Japanese passports are all eligible to apply for holiday working visas.

There is a processing fee of £55 for each holiday working visa. This can be paid by cheque to 'Commonwealth of Australia'. Contact your bank for the correct rate of exchange at the time of your application and convert the sum accordingly.

Types of work available

Nothing should be discounted but the major areas of employment are factory work, farm work, fishing, fruit-picking, hospitality, labouring and mining.

Official employment agencies

The official employment agency in Australia is the **Commonwealth Employment Service (CES)**. Holders of holiday working visas can take advantage of the CES offices around the country and the services they have to offer. For jobs in catering, fruit-picking and labouring the CES will either be able to offer you specific jobs or, failing that, they will be able to direct you to the areas where

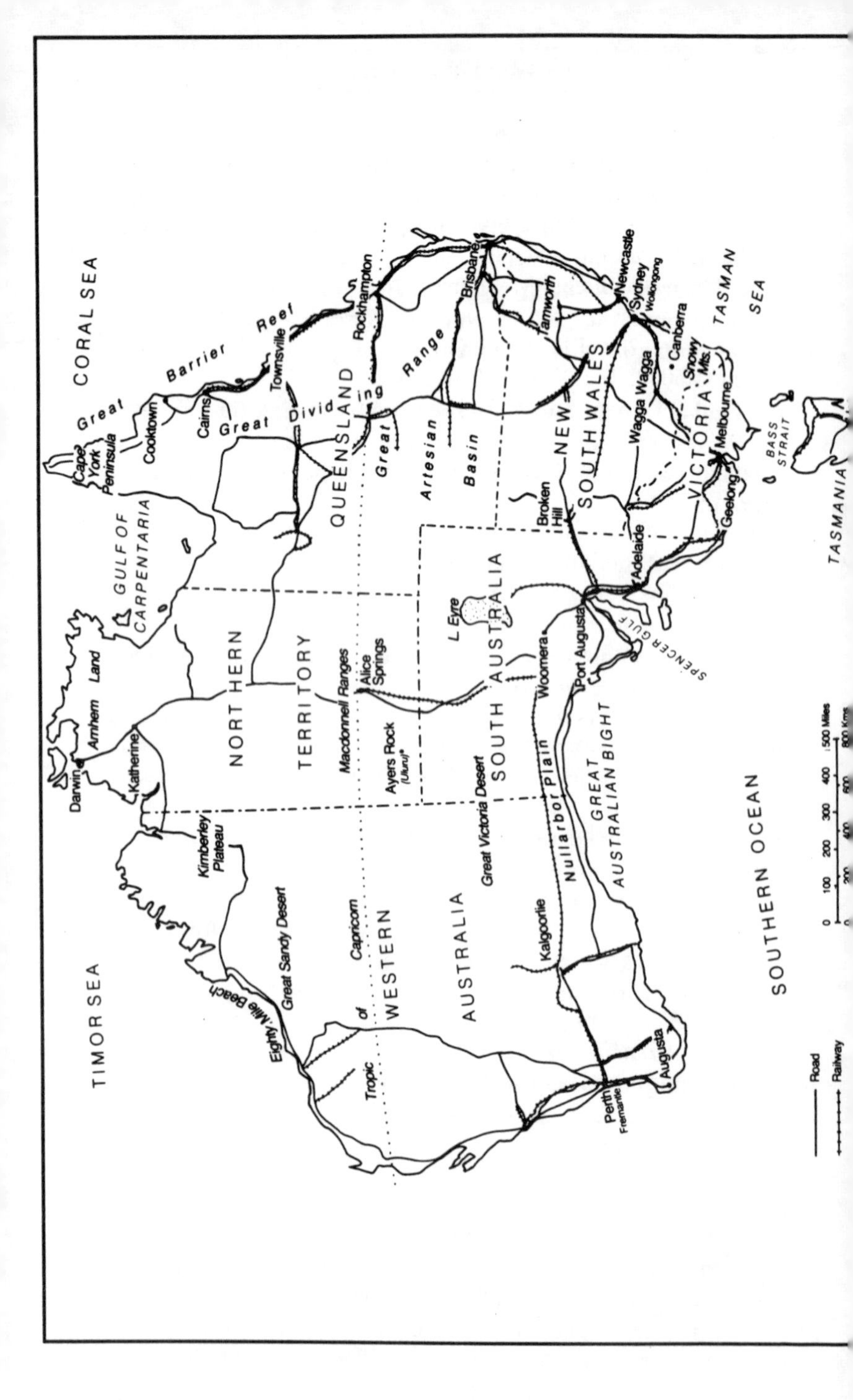

Fig. 6. Map of Australia.

workers are most needed.

Although casual employees can use any CES, there are some that cater specifically for their needs:

CES Templine, 9th Floor, Santos House, 215 Adelaide Street, Brisbane, Queesland 4002. Tel: 07 229 5188.

CES, 128 Bourke Street, Melbourne, Victoria 3000. Tel: 03 666 1222.

CES Templine, 2nd Floor, 45 Grenfell Street, Adelaide, South Australia 5000. Tel: 08 231 9070.

CES, 818–820 George Street, Railway Square, Sydney, NSW 2000. Tel: 02 281 6088.

CES, 1st Floor, 186 St. George's Terrace, Perth, Western Australia 6000. Tel: 09 325 6155.

CES Templine, 1st Floor, 40 Cavenagh Street, Darwin, Northern Territory 0801. Tel: 089 46 4866.

CES, 175 Collins Street, Hobart, Tasmania 7000. Tel: 002 20 4068.

Private employment agencies

Australian Capital Territory/Canberra

Keydata Temps, 10 Cohen Street, Belconnen. Tel: 062 251 5133. Specialists in temporary staff covering; keyboard operators, word processing operators, secretarial, clerical, receptionists and personal assistants.

Templine, 33 Ainslie Avenue, Canberra City. Tel: 062 274 4000. Specialists in temporary staff covering; word processing operators, secretarial, reception and clerical.

Tourism and Hospitality Service, 39 Jardine Street, Kingston. Tel: 062 295 3633. Permanent and temporary positions for all areas of the hospitality industry.

University of Canberra Student Employment Office, University of Canberra, Kirinari Street, Bruce, Canberra City. Casual and part-time opportunities for a wide range of workers.

New South Wales

The majority of employment agencies in Sydney have more than one office in the city. The addresses given here are for the most central offices to the city centre. For branch offices, look in the *Yellow Pages* for Sydney.

Brook Street, 4 Martin Place, Sydney. Tel: 02 233 1000. Permanent and temporary staff covering; executive secretaries, personal assistants, word processing operators, data entry operators, receptionists, hospitality support staff, clerical staff, accounting, computer, sales and marketing, insurance, legal and medical.

Centacom, 72 Pitt Street, Sydney. Tel: 902 231 5555. Secretaries, receptionists, word processor operators, clerical office, sales and accountancy support.

Drake Personnel, 255 George Street, Sydney. Tel: 02 231 6644. Typists, secretaries, word processor operators, data entry operators, clerks, bookkeepers, receptionists, telephonists, accounting machine operators and computer operators.

Professional Catering Staff, 2 Grosvenor Street, Bondi Junction, Sydney. Tel: 02 389 0155. All areas of the catering industry.

Travel Staff, 64 Castlereagh, Sydney. Tel: 02 233 1466. Permanent and temporary staff covering; travel executives, consultants, reservations, secretarial and support staff.

University of Sydney Graduate Employment Service, Arundel Street, Forest Lodge, Sydney. Tel: 02 692 3481. Casual and temporary employment for students and graduates.

Queensland

Brook Street, 145 Eagle Street, Brisbane. Tel: 07 832 3844. Permanent and temporary staff covering; executive secretaries, personal assistants, word processing operators, data entry operators, receptionists, hospitality support staff, clerical staff, accounting, computing, sales and marketing, insurance, legal and medical.

Capablestaff, 5th Floor, Eagle House, 82 Eagle Street, Brisbane, GPO Box 2174 Brisbane. Tel: 07 221 9661. Permanent and temporary staff covering; executives, secretarial, engineering, marketing, scientific, accounting, computing, trades, sales and training.

Food and Beverage Staff Placement, Timothy's Catering Service, 919 Sandgate Road, Clayfield, Brisbane. Tel: 07 862 2051. Managers, chefs, bar staff, waiters, cooks and bookkeepers.

Kelly Hospitality Recruitment, Level 5, 135 Wickham Terrace, Spring Hill. Tel: 07 832 2244. Executives, chefs, management, front office, housekeeping, financial, administrative, bar staff, floor staff and cleaning staff.

Manpower, 307 Queen Street, Brisbane. Tel: 07 221 0766. Permanent and temporary staff covering; office work and sales, warehouse staff, fork-lift truck drivers, labourers, truck drivers and offsiders, process workers and tradesmen.

Mitchell Consultants, 101 Wickham Terrace, Spring Hill. Tel: 07 832 4700. Permanent, temporary and contract staff covering; office, professional, sales, engineering, trades and computing.

South Australia

Hospitality Staffing, 2nd Floor, Wyatt House, 115 Grenfell Streeet, Adelaide. Tel: 08 224 6161. Specialist recruitment for hotels, motels, restaurants, clubs and functions.

Metier, 45 King Street, Adelaide. Tel: 08 231 4777. Permanent and temporary staff covering; secretarial, word processing and office positions.

Oak Industrial, Suite 4, 155 Fullarton Road, Rose Park, South Australia 5067. Permanent, temporary and contract staff covering; manufacturing, engineering, maintenance drafting and technical.

Quality Staff, 29 Marryatt Street, Port Adelaide. Tel: 08 341 2345. Permanent and temporary staff covering; executives, sales, secretarial and clerical.

Victoria

A La Carte Staff Agency, 343 Little Collins Street, Melbourne. Tel: 03 670 7844. Permanent, temporary and emergency covering; management, front office, executive chefs and cooks, waiting staff, bar staff, kitchen hands, canteen assistants and housemaids.

Australia Wide Personnel, 79 Mahoneys Road, Forest Hill. Tel: 03 877 2322. Permanent, temporary and contract staff covering; engineering, production, technical, sales, marketing, office support, word processing, accounting, administration and management.

Cartell Personnel, Suite 314, 3rd Floor 343 Lit Collins, Melbourne. Tel: 03 670 5661. Permanent and temporary staff for all areas of office work.

Carver and Associates, 2nd Floor 37 Queen Street, Melbourne. Tel: 03 614 7211. Permanent, temporary and support staff covering; word processing, secretarial, data entry and accounts clerks.

Centacom Staff, 51 Elizabeth Street, Melbourne. Tel: 03 629 6291. Permanent and temporary staff covering; secretaries, receptionists, word processor operators, clerical, office, sales and accountancy support.

Kelly Services, 2nd Floor 454 Collins Street, Melbourne. Tel: 03 670 9966. Permanent and temporary staff covering; secretarial, office support, clerical, accountants, bookkeepers, insurance staff, finance staff, PC operators, receptionists, sales and marketing.

Western Australia

Drake, 108 George's Terrace, Perth. Tel: 09 321 9911. Permanent or temporary staff covering; secretaries, word processing, taxation, auditing, management and bookkeeping.

Hospitality Personnel, Suite 17, The Russell Centre, 159 Adelaide Terrace, Perth. Tel: 09 221 2468. Permanent and temporary staff for hospitality staff in hotels, pubs, clubs and restaurants.

Pollitt's Employment Agency, 251 Adelaide Terrace, Perth. Tel: 09 325 2544. Permanent and temporary staff for all areas of the hospitality business.

Success Personnel, 26 St. George's Terrace, Perth. Tel: 09 221 1522. Permanent and temporary staff for all categories.

Superior Personnel, Suite 6, 678 Beaufort Street, Mount Lawley, WA. Tel: 09 370 3121. Permanent and temporary staff for office work and word processing.

Tomorrow's Staff (incorporating Catertemp), 7th Floor, City Arcade Tower, 207 Murray Street, Perth 6000. Tel: 09 321 6391. Twenty-four hour relief service for all hospitality and catering staff.

Work opportunities

Fruit-picking

This is traditionally a boom area for casual employment. Not only that, but it is a good way for the overseas worker to see a side of Australian life which they would not see in a big city. The nature of the work is hard and dirty and the financial rewards vary from the mediocre to the excellent. To find fruit-picking work you should go to the CES office nearest to the area in which you want to work. They will advise you on job availability.

Due to problems in other sectors of the economy more and more people are now turning to fruit-picking for a living. This means there are less places for casual workers from abroad. This at least is the official line you will hear from the CES. Unofficially, the nature of fruit-picking and the conditions under which the workers live mean that pickers are frequently walking off the job. The best way to land a picking job is to go to a fruit growing area and start knocking on a few farm doors. People have even been approached in the street in fruit-picking towns and offered jobs. The best time is towards the end of the season when the growers are getting desperate to get their crops in and the pickers are getting fed up with their task.

Fruit-picking as a means of employment during a year in Australia is not only a good idea from the financial point of view, it also has the big advantage of being the type of work that you would not come across at home. Making use of a holiday working visa is not so much about how much you earn but rather what you do. Fruit-picking will be an experience you will never forget, no matter how hard you try.

Other crops
All Australian states, with the exception of the Northern Territory, have fruit-picking and, if you are so inclined, you can pick different crops from January to December. Crops as diverse as asparagus and cotton chipping can be harvested, while grapes remain one of the most popular options. There are CES offices in all fruit-picking areas and these should be tried first to see if there is any work in the area. Farms should also be approached individually as pickers come and go with remarkable regularity.

Hospitality
This is one area in which people on holiday working visas have traditionally found a variety of casual work. Whether it is as a potwasher (dishwasher) in a five-star hotel or a bar person at the tourist resort at Ayers Rock, catering staff are in demand in all areas of the Australian hospitality industry.

Although experience is not always necessary for this type of work it does pay to look clean, tidy and respectable when applying for jobs. If you do have experience as a barperson, a chef or a waiter/waitress then take references with you to convince employers of your suitability. Since numerous other people will be looking for the same types of jobs as yourself you will need a certain amount of luck and, at times, a lot of determination to land a job in hospitality.

Check local newspapers and the CES and if there are no suitable vacancies then go knocking on some doors. It is conceivable that you could spend several days without success but do not become down-hearted. Keep trying and do not be afraid to go to the same place two, three or four times — workers are frequently leaving or being fired from bars and restaurants and if you arrive at one of those moments then you could be in luck.

Factory work
If you have a high boredom threshold then you could consider working in a factory packing the likes of pineapples or soap. A good source of information about job availability are fellow travellers who have 'Been there and done it'. It is also worth following the fruit-picking cycle — a lot of this produce will be packed for consumption in other parts of the country or overseas. The pay tends to be good for this type of work but you may be driven crazy if you do it for too long.

Fishing
There are some jobs to be had on prawn fishing vessels out of Broome,

Darwin, Cairns and Townsville. The main jobs for men are net-mending and prawn-sorting, while women are usually taken on board as cooks. A set of good sea-legs and a willingness to work hard are the best qualifications for this type of work but it is worth remembering that you may be at sea for several weeks at one time. Payment is in the form of a fixed wage or a share of the catch. Since the number of prawns being caught is smaller than it used to be a more stable option is to take the former. If you are a female member of crew you should make it perfectly clear what your role on board is going to include — and, more importantly, what your role is not going to include.

You can look for this type of work through the CES, or approach privately-owned boats or large companies, although these will probably tell you that you have to be a member of a seaman's union.

Jackaroo/Jillaroo
For people with farm experience of some description it may be possible to get a job as a jackaroo or a jillaroo (a sheep station assistant). Although it sounds romantic the chances are that you will not be riding across the outback on your trusty steed. In reality there can be a lot of sitting around on a sheep station — if not you will be doing all the jobs that no one else can be bothered with. Ask someone who has done it before you commit yourself.

Labouring
This area of employment is being hit harder than most as a result of the recession. As the building trade contracts so the need for labourers dwindles. You could try visiting building sites to see if there is any work going but the best bet is to go to a relevant CES *early* in the morning. If there is any need for labourers they will be picked from the pool of men who gather at or before 6 am. This is done on a day to day basis but it could lead to some useful contacts.

Mining
The more robust and adventurous could try and find work in the mining areas of North Western Australia or the Northern Territory. Due to recent contraction in the industry there are few jobs advertised in the local newspapers or CES so it is a case of going to the mines themselves. Since they can be hundreds of miles from any major city this is a considerable risk if you do not find a job.

Temporary job rating
Very good. Taking the plunge to go to Australia is an important decision but once you have done this you should concentrate your efforts on being as well prepared as possible for finding work once

you arrive. The Australian employment world is more concerned with whether you can do the job rather than what qualifications you have or your accent.

New Zealand

New Zealand High Commission, Immigration Service, New Zealand House, 80 Haymarket, London SW1Y 4TE. Tel: (071) 973 0366.

Visa/work permit requirements
UK citizens do not require a visa for a visit of up to 6 months in New Zealand. However, a work permit is required if you intend to undertake any kind of employment. These should be applied for from the local office of the Immigration Service once you are in New Zealand and have been offered a job. This is expensive, £40 for a temporary work visa, and so many people just obtain a tax number instead (simply by asking for one at the Inland Revenue Department) and give this to employers.

Types of work available
Fruit-picking, hospitality and voluntary work.

Temporary work rating
Moderate. From a distance the work permit regulations can seem a bit daunting but if you get to New Zealand you will probably find that there are a sufficient number of employers who are willing to overlook the need for official paperwork. Fruit-picking and hospitality work can be found and there is not the same cut-throat competition as there is in some parts of Australia.

MIDDLE EAST

Israel is the most realistic option for the temporary job seeker in the Middle East.

Israel

Israeli Embassy, 2 Palace Green, London W8 4QB. Tel: (071) 957 9500.

Visa/work permit requirements
UK citizens require work permits for all types of work in Israel.

Types of work available
Although there are some openings for au pairs and archaeological

work the main forms of temporary work are found on kibbutzim and moshavim. As with most things it seems to be getting harder for people to find places on these traditional havens for the temporary worker and it is advised that a place is obtained before leaving for Israel.

Prospective employers

Kibbutz work

A kibbutz (from the Hebrew word for group) is a voluntary, democratic community where people live and work together on a non-profit, non-competitive basis. Private property is limited to personal possessions.

There are currently over 270 kibbutzim in Israel, varying in size from 100 members to 2,000 members. In total, kibbutz members number 120,000, which represents approximately 2.8 per cent of Israel's population.

All kibbutzim have permanent members — kibbutzniks — but they all take on volunteer workers who live and work on the kibbutz for anything between five weeks and three months (although this can easily be extended). The kibbutzniks have their own living units but meals are taken together in the communal hall.

Points to consider before you go to a kibbutz as a volunteer worker:

1. You must be in good physical and mental shape.
2. You will have to work long hours, six days a week, doing whatever jobs you are assigned. This could be working in the kitchens, picking melons or raising chickens.
3. You will be sleeping in cramped, spartan conditions.
4. You will have to conform to the rules and regulations of the kibbutz for the period you are living there.
5. Although you will be doing the same work as the kibbutzniks you will be treated like an outsider if you do not accept their way of life.

How to apply to be a volunteer

There are organisations in the UK that deal with placing volunteers with kibbutzim:

Giltours (UK) Limited, 16 Gloucester Place, London W1H 3AW. Tel: (071) 935 1701.

Kibbutz Representatives, 1A Accommodation Road, London NW11 8EP. Tel: (081) 458 9235.

Project 67 Limited, 10 Hatton Garden, London EC1N 8AH. Tel: (071) 831 7626.

A registration fee of approximately £40 has to be paid when

applying to a kibbutz through these organisations.

Applying in Israel

Most people who have made their own way to Israel and applied to kibbutzim through agencies in Tel Aviv agree that this is just as effective, and cheaper, than going through an agency in Britain. However, since the demand for kibbutzim volunteers can fluctuate from year to year it is a good idea looking at the merits of both methods.

If you do travel independently to Israel and apply on the spot then you should go to various agencies in Tel Aviv. These are in effect recruitment centres for the kibbutzim.

Takam (United Kibbutz Movement), 82 Hayarkon Street, POB 26131, Tel Aviv. Tel: 03-655207/651710.

Ha'Kibbutz Ha'Artzi, 118 Hayarkon Street, Tel Aviv 63573. Tel: 03 223703/225924.

Moshav/Kibbutz Volunteers Center, 5 Tiomkin, Tel Aviv 65783. Tel: 625806.

The agencies will charge you a registration fee and arrange compulsory insurance.

If you do not want to do this then you can approach the kibbutzim directly. This is a bit hit and miss but several travellers have reported being given places in this fashion. For both methods you will need to have the relevant working papers with you — currently a B–4 volunteer visa.

Moshavim

These are similar to kibbutzim in concept but they differ in that the members can own their machinery and houses. The work can be harder than on a kibbutz but in return the worker receives a basic wage for his efforts — approximately £200 a month. There is also more opportunity to mix with people outside the moshav.

You can apply in Britain through Giltours (UK) Limited and Project 67 Limited (see above).

Archaeology

Ayala Travel, 13 Hazvi Street, Jerusalem 94386, Israel. Tel: 02 381233. Run holiday digs throughout Israel.

Department of Classical Studies, Professor M. Gichon, Division of Archaeology, Yad Avner, Ramat Aviv, 69978 Tel Aviv, Israel. Require volunteers for digs at Horvat Eqed and Emmaus.

The Hebrew University of Jerusalem, The Director, Institute of Archaeology, Mount Scopus, Jerusalem 91905, Israel. Run digs throughout Israel.

Israel Antiquities Authority, PO Box 586, Rockerfeller Museum, Jerusalem 91004, Israel. Tel: 02 292607. Require volunteers for a variety of digs throughout Israel.

Jewish National Fund, Eli Shenhav, 11 Zvi Shapira Street, Tel Aviv 64538. Require volunteers for a dig at Binyamina.

Au pairs

Anglia Agency, 70 Southsea Avenue, Leigh-on-Sea, Essex. Tel: (0702) 471648.

Helping Hands Au Pair and Domestic Agency, 30 Rutland Avenue, Thorpe Bay, Essex SS1 2XJ. Tel: (0702) 602067.

Star Au Pair International, 16 Michal Street, Tel Aviv 63261, Israel.

Students Abroad Limited, 11 Milton View, Hitchin, Herts SG4 0QD. Tel: (0462) 438909.

Temporary work rating

Good — but only if you are interested in working within a limited area of officially organised work. Freelance work does take place in Israel but it is the exception rather than the rule.

NORTH AMERICA

USA

Embassy of the United States of America, 24 Grosvenor Square, London W1A 1AE. Tel: (071) 499 9000.

Visa Section, 5 Upper Grosvenor Street, London W1A 2JB. Tel: (0891) 200290.

Visa/work permit requirements

Although UK citizens do not always require visas to visit the United States a working visa is required by anyone who wants to work in the States. For the purposes of official employment these must be obtained before arrival in the US. The two types of visa that relate to temporary work are: the J–1 visa for people on Exchange Visitor Programmes (EVP) such as BUNAC or Camp America; and the H–2 temporary worker visa for people who have a pre-arranged temporary job with an American employer. The employment situation in the US is such that most people who work there officially do so through various EVPs and so have a J–1 visa. Obtaining an H–2 visa can be a long and tiresome task and can only be done if you have a job to go to.

Alternatively there is a massive network of illegal workers in the States — some people from Britain have been working there illegally for over 20 years. The range of jobs available is similar to that in

Australia and thousands of workers from the UK have found jobs without having work visas. The down side of this is that your employer can be fined if he employs illegal labour and you will be deported. It is therefore not recommended. The choice is up to the individual but if you do work illegally make sure you are well insured.

Types of work available
Archaeology, au pair, summer camps and voluntary work. There are thousands of temporary job opportunities offered by various organisations. For a comprehensive list consult *Summer Jobs USA*, distributed by Vacation Work, 9 Park End Street, Oxford OX1 1HJ.

Prospective employers
Archaeology
Earthwatch Europe, Belsyre Court, 57 Woodstock Road, Oxford. Tel: (0865) 311600. Run a wide range of research programmes in various areas of the States.
Foundation For Field Research, PO Box 2010, Alpine, California 91903, USA. Run digs in the southern areas of the States.
Mission San Antonio Archaeological School, Social Sciences Department, California Polytechnic State University, San Luis Obispo, CA 93407, USA. Require volunteers to conduct research into Spanish colonial archaeology.
Mount Clare Restoration Office, Carroll Park, 1500 Washington Boulevard, Baltimore, MD 21230, USA. Require archaeological volunteers to work in Baltimore.

Au pairs
The following agencies can place au pairs on US Government authorised programmes.
Academy Au Pair Agency Limited, Glenlea, Dulwich Common, London SE21 7ES. Tel: (081) 299 4599.
American Institute For Foreign Study, Au Pair in America Programme, 37 Queens Gate, London SW7 5HR. Tel: (071) 581 2730.
Avalon Agency, Thursley House, 53 Station Road, Shalford, Guildford, Surrey GU4 8HA. Tel: (0483) 63640.
CBR Au Pair, 63 Foregate Street, Worcester WR1 1EE. Tel: (0905) 26671.
The Experiment In International Living, Au Pair Homestay USA, Otesaga, West Malvern Road, Malvern, Worcestershire WR14 4EN. Tel: (0684) 562577.
Just The Job Employment Agency, 8 Musters Road, West

Fig. 7. Map of the USA.

Bridgford, Nottingham NG2 5PL. Tel: (0602) 813224.
Students Abroad Limited, 11 Milton View, Hitchin, Herts SG4 0QD. Tel: (0462) 438909.

Summer camps
See Chapter 4.

Voluntary work
For a full list of voluntary opportunities in the States you could get a copy of *Volunteer! The Comprehensive Guide to Voluntary Service in the US and Abroad*, Council on International Educational Exchange, Publications Department, 205 E 42nd St, New York, NY 10017, USA.
Appalachian Trail Conference, PO Box 10, Newport, Virginia 24128, USA. Use volunteers to help maintain the Appalachian Trail.
The Sioux Indian YMCA, PO Box 218, Dupree, South Dakota 57623, USA. Require volunteers to work in reservations in South Dakota.
Student Conservation Association Inc, PO Box 550, Charlestown, NH 03603, USA. Require volunteers to help conserve over 200 national parks in the States.
University Research Expeditions Program, University of California, Desk M11, Berkeley, CA 94720, USA. Require volunteers to help with research into natural and social sciences.
Winant-Clayton Volunteers Assoication, 38 Newark Street, London E1 2AA. Provide volunteers to work on city community projects in the eastern states.

Temporary work rating
Good. Every worker will have to decide whether they want to work with an officially authorised organisation or go freelance and work illegally. There are numerous opportunities for both methods but the drawbacks of working illegally should be kept in mind.

Canada
Canadian High Commission, Macdonald House, 1 Grosvenor Square, London W1X 0AB. Tel: (071) 629 9492.
Immigration Section, 38 Grosvenor Street, London W1X 0AA. Tel: (071) 409 2071.

Visa/work permit requirements
UK Citizens do not require visas to visit Canada. However, people

who wish to work in Canada require a work permit which must be gained prior to entry into the country. In recent years work authorizations have been introduced to allow a specific number of students to work temporarily in Canada. For students who have a pre-arranged job they can apply for the work authorization through the Canadian High Commission. Alternatively, students who want to find a job when they arrive in Canada can apply through BUNAC's Camp Canada (see Chapter 4).

Types of work available

Au pair, fruit-picking, hospitality and voluntary work.

Prospective employers

Au pairs

Academy Au Pair Agency Limited, Glenlea, Dulwich Common, London SE21 7ES. Tel: (081) 299 4599.

Anglia Agency, 70 Southsea Avenue, Leigh-on-Sea, Essex. Tel: (0702) 471648.

Anglo Pair Agency, 40 Wavertree Road, Streatham Hill, London SW2 3SP. Tel: (081) 674 3605.

Avalon Agency, Thursley House, 53 Station Road, Shalford, Guildford, Surrey GU4 8HA. Tel: (0483) 63640.

Nannies Unlimited Inc, PO Box 5864, Station A., Calgary, Alberta T2H 1X4.

Students Abroad Limited, 11 Milton View, Hitchin, Herts SG4 0QD. Tel: (0462) 438909.

Fruit-picking

The main area for fruit-picking is the Okanagan valley in British Columbia. The crops include apples, apricots, cherries, peaches and pears. There is also some fruit-picking in Ontario. Tobacco is also harvested in Ontario and this is a popular choice for temporary workers.

Voluntary work

Canadian Parks Service, National Volunteer Coordinator, 25 Eddy Street, Ottawa, Ontario K1A 9H3. Tel: 819 994 5127. Require volunteers to work in national parks, historic sites and canals.

Frontiers Foundation Inc, Operation Beaver, 2615 Danforth Avenue, Suite 293, Toronto, Ontario M4C 1L6. Tel: 416 690 3930. Help improve the way of life for disadvantaged communities.

International Agricultural Exchange Association, YFC Centre, National Agricultural Centre, Stoneleigh Park, Kenilworth,

Warwickshire CV8 2LG. Tel: (0203) 696578.

Willing Workers On Organic Fams RR2, Carlson Road S18 C9, Nelson, British Columbia V1L 5P5, Canada. Require volunteers to help organic farmers.

Temporary work rating

Good — but only if you can arrange a work authorization permit or work with a voluntary organisation. If you cannot do this then the likelihood is that you will have to work illegally. This can be done and there is work to be found. However, the authorities come down on illegal workers very heavily, and pursue them with considerable enthusiasm, so it is best to avoid illegal working.

SOUTH AND CENTRAL AMERICA

Embassies

Argentine Embassy, 53 Hans Place, London SW1X 0LA. Tel: (071) 584 6494.

Belize High Commission, 10 Harcourt House, 19a Cavendish Square, London W1M 9AD. Tel: (071) 499 9728.

Bolivian Embassy, 106 Eaton Square, London SW1W 9AD. Tel: (071) 235 4248/2257.

Brazilian Embassy, 32 Green Street, Mayfair, London W1Y 4AT. Tel: (071) 499 0877.

Chilean Embassy, 12 Devonshire Street, London W1N 2DS. Tel: (071) 580 6392.

Costa Rica Embassy, 5 Harcourt House, 19a Cavendish Square, London W1M 9AD. Tel: (071) 495 3985.

Cuban Embassy, 167 High Holburn, London WC1V 6PA. Tel: (071) 240 2488.

Ecuador Embassy, Flat 3b, 3 Hans Crescent, Knightsbridge, London SW1X 0LS. Tel: (071) 584 1367.

Mexican Embassy, 42 Hertford Street, Mayfair, London W1Y 7TF. Tel: (071) 499 8586.

Nicaraguan Embassy, 8 Gloucester Road, London SW7 4PP. Tel: (071) 584 4365.

Paraguay Embassy, Braemar Lodge, Cornwall Gardens, London SW7 4AQ. TEl: (071) 937 1253.

Peruvian Embassy, 52 Sloane Street, London SW1X 9SP. Tel: (071) 235 1917/2545.

Overview

The opportunities for paid temporary work in South American countries are limited almost exclusively to Teaching English as a Foreign Language (TEFL) and voluntary work. There is a thriving TEFL industry in most South American countries and it is possible, and in many cases advisable, to find work once you are there so you can assess the situation more accurately. As long as you can speak English, and are not too gullible, you should be able to teach your way around South America.

Permits

Strictly speaking, work permits are required for temporary workers in South America but they are difficult to obtain and the vast majority of travellers do not bother.

TEFL openings

English can be taught in all South American countries but two of the most popular are Chile and Mexico.

Chile

People wishing to advertise their TEFL talents can do so in a variety of newspapers in Chile: *Ya*, a supplement of *El Mercurio*; *La Epoca*; *La Tercera* and *El Rastro*.

- Language schools:

  Concord Chile Inc, Nueva York 57, Of. 501, Santiago.

  Fischer English Institute, Cirujano Guzman 49, Providencia, Santiago.

  Lang International Limited, Bucarest 046, Dp. E, Providencia, Santiago.

  Sheila May's, Napoleon 3070, Las Condes, Santiago.

  San Marsalli, Avenida Los Leones 1095, Providencia, Santiago.

Mexico

Check the advertisements in the English language newspaper *The News*. Numerous companies advertise for people to teach their workers English and their primary concern is that you are a native English speaker. There could also be possibilities at: Culturlingua Language Center, Plaza Jardinadas, Local 24 y 25, Zamora, Michoacan.

Conservation

Coral Cay Conservation Limited, The Sutton Business Centre, Restmor Way, Wallington, Surrey SM6 7AH. Sends expeditions to Belize to check on pollution levels on the Great Atlantic Barrier Reef. Volunteers must be members of the British Sub-Aqua Club or have an equivalent certificate from a recognised training agency.

Earthwatch Europe, Belsyre Court, 57 Woodstock Road, Oxford. Tel: (0865) 311600. Organises expenditions to South America that deal with a wide range of conservation issues.

Genesis II Cloud Forest Regeneration Project, Aptdo. 655, 7.050 Cartago, Costa Rica. A Canadian organisation dedicated to preserving a high altitude cloud forest. Volunteers pay at least $100 a week and competition is fierce.

University Research Expeditions Program, University of California, Desk M11, Berkeley CA 94720, USA. Runs research programmes in natural and social sciences. Operate in Costa Rica and Ecuador.

Voluntary work

American Friends Service Committee Inc, Personnel Department, 1501 Cherry Street, Philadelphia, Pennsylvania 19102, USA. A Quaker organisation that undertakes relief work, principally in Mexico.

Amigos de las Americas, 5618 Star Lane, Houston, Texas, USA. Aims to improve community health throughout South America.

Atlantis, c/o Ned Addis, Icononzo, Tolima, Columbia. Runs communes, and willing workers are welcome.

Cuba Solidarity Campaign, Jose Marti International Work Brigade, Latin America House, Priory House, Kingsgate Place, London NW6. Tel: (071) 388 1429. Runs agricultural and construction work camps in Havana province.

Escuela de Enfermeria Stella Maris, Apartado Postal 28, Zacapu, Michoacan, Mexico 58680. Volunteers required to help at a nursing school in Mexico.

Federacion de Organizaciones Voluntarias de Costa Rica, PO Box 7-3070-1000, San Jose, Costa Rica. An umbrella organisation for voluntary groups in Costa Rica.

Nicaragua Solidarity Campaign, 129 Seven Sisters Road, London N7 7OG. Organises expeditions to Nicaragua to assist agricultural cooperatives and environmental organisations in the north of the country.

Servicio Educativo de Turismo de Los Estudiantes, y la Juventad de Mexico AC (SETEJ), Hamburgo 273, Colonio Juarez, Mexico City 06600 DF, Mexico. Organises six week long work camps throughout Mexico.

Voluntarios en Accion (VEA), PO Box 3556, La Paz, Bolivia. Aid rural education in Bolivia.

Temporary work rating

Moderate. Definitely an area for the seasoned traveller/worker. Working with a recognised aid agency is probably the best bet if you want to go through official channels. For the freelance job seeker teaching English is definitely the most likely avenue.

AFRICA

Embassies

Algerian Embassy, 54 Holland Park, London W11 3RS. Tel: (071) 221 7800.

Egyptian Embassy, 26 South Street, London W1Y 8EL. Tel: (071) 499 2401.

Kenyan High Commission, 45 Portland Place, London W1N 4AS. Tel: (071) 636 2371/5.

Lesotho High Commission, 10 Collingham Road, London SW5 0NR. Tel: (071) 373 8581/2.

Malawi High Commission, 33 Grosvenor Street, London W1X 0DE. Tel: (071) 491 4172.

Moroccan Embassy, 49 Queen's Gate Gardens, London SW7 5NE. Tel: (071) 581 5001.

Nigerian High Commission, Nigeria House, 9 Northumberland Avenue, London WC2N 5BX. Tel: (071) 839 1244.

Sierra Leone High Commission, 33 Portland Place, London W1N 3AG. Tel: (071) 636 6483.

South African Embassy, South Africa House, Trafalgar Square, London WC2N 5DP. Tel: (071) 930 4488.

Tanzanian High Commission, 43 Hertford Street, London W1Y 8DB. Tel: (071) 499 8951.

Tunisian Embassy, 29 Princes Gate, London SW7 1QG. Tel: (071) 584 8117.

Zaire Embassy, 26 Chesham Place, London SW1X 8HH. Tel: (071) 235 6137.

Zimbabwe High Commission, Zimbabwe House, 429 Strand, London WC2R 0SA. Tel: (071) 836 7755.

Overview

Finding a job as a dishwasher or a fruit picker in Africa is about as likely as a snow flurry in the Sahara. However, there are numerous openings for Teaching English as a Foreign Language (TEFL), adventure travel work, and voluntary work. With a large supply of local labour, and prohibitively restrictive work permit requirements, most African countries do not offer many types of temporary work. People who do find work there either do so by working illegally or through a recognised voluntary organisation operating in Africa.

The one notable exception to this is South Africa. If you are willing to look beyond the political problems then it could be worth a visit from the employment point of view. The official line is that work permits will only be given if you can prove the job you are going to do cannot be undertaken by a South African citizen. In reality personal contacts are more important and travellers in South Africa have worked illegally in occupations as diverse as alarm salesmen and hairdressing models.

Types of employment

Adventure companies

Exodus Expeditions, 9 Weir Road, London SW12 0LT. Tel: (081) 675 7996. Organises truck tours through Africa and also adventure holidays in Kenya, Morocco and Tanzania. People wishing to work as drivers or leaders must be aged 25-30 and have an HGV/PSV licence.

Conservation

Earthwatch Europe, Belsyre Court, 57 Woodstock Road, Oxford OX2 6HU. Tel: (0865) 311600. Gives support to researchers in a wide range of conservation work in various areas of Africa.

Gormorgor Agricultural Development Organisation, c/o Njala University College, Private Mail Bag, Freetown, Sierra Leone. Runs projects to upgrade subsistence farming throughout Sierra Leone. Some farm experience is usually required.

TEFL openings

Opportunities for teaching English vary greatly from country to country and some nations actually recruit through their embassies abroad. It may be worth getting in touch with the Education Attaché of the relevant embassy. Missionary organisations also employ people to teach English in Africa. Two of them are:

Volunteer Missionary Movement (VMM), Comboni House, London Road, Sunningdale, Ascot, Berks SL5 0JX. Employs qualified teachers to work for two years in countries ranging from Kenya to Zimbabwe.

Christians Abroad, 1 Stockwell Green, London SW9 9HP. Uses volunteers to teach in Malawi and Zimbabwe.

As far as TEFL is concerned Africa is one area where it really pays to use your initiative. Schools in many countries are short of teachers and if you can turn up and convince them that you are the one to teach English you may be taken on. A professional attitude and a degree will help you enormously and probably ensure that you receive a higher wage. If you are in a country and want to try teaching English it would be a good idea to try and find someone who has done it and pick their brains for the do's and don'ts.

Work camp organisations:

Alliance des Unions Chretiennes de Jeune Gens du Cameroun, BP 89, Douala, Cameroun. Tel: (42) 7099.

Kenya Voluntary Development Association, PO Box 48902, Nairobi, Kenya.

Lesotho Workcamps Association, PO Box 6, Linare Road, Maseru 100, Lesotho. Tel: (050) 314862.

Union Marocaine des Associations de Chantiers, BP 455, Rabat, Morocco.

Voluntary Workcamp Association of Nigeria, PO Box 2189, Ebute-Metta, Lagos, Nigeria.

Nigeria Voluntary Service Association, PO Box 11837, Ibadan, Nigeria.

African Voluntary Service of Sierra Leone, PMB 717, Freetown, Sierra Leone.

Tunisian Association of Voluntary Work, Maison du Parti, La Kasbah, Boulevard 9 Avril, Tunis, Tunisia. Tel: 264899.

For more information about work camps in Africa it would be worthwhile to contact one of the following organisation in the UK:

Concordia (Youth Service Volunteers) Ltd, Recruitment Secretary, 8 Brunswick Place, Hove, Sussex BN3 1ET. Tel: (0273) 772086.

Quaker International Social Projects, Friends House, Euston Road, London NW1 2BJ.

United Nations Association, International Youth Service, Temple of Peace, Cathays Park, Cardiff CF1 3AP. Tel: (0222) 223088.

Temporary job rating

Moderate. Determined teachers of English should always be able to earn a crust in Africa and there is always a need for voluntary workers. It is best to approach the prospect of finding temporary work in Africa with an open mind. If you go there expecting to find work then you may be disappointed; if you go there hoping to pick up what you can while you are travelling then you may end up working for several months.

ASIA

Embassies

Bangladesh High Commission, 28 Queen's Gate, London SW7 5JA. Tel: (071) 584 0081.
Embassy of the People's Republic of China, 49-51 Portland Place, London W1N 3AH. Tel: (071) 636 9375/5726.
Hong Kong High Commission, 125 Pall Mall, 5th Floor, London SW1Y 5EA. Tel: (071) 930 4775.
Indian High Commission, India House, Aldwych, London WC2B 4NA. Tel: (071) 826 8484.
Indonesian Embassy, 38 Grosvenor Square, London W1X 9AD. Tel: (071) 499 7661.
Japanese Embassy, 46 Grosvenor Street, London W1X 0BA. Tel: (071) 493 6030.
Korean Embassy, 4 Palace Gate, London W8 5NF. Tel: (071) 581 0247.
Malaysian Embassy, 45 Belgrave Square, London SW1X 8QT. Tel: (071) 235 8033.
Royal Nepalese Embassy, 12a Kensington Palace Gardens, London W8 4QU. Tel: (071) 229 1594/6231.
Pakistan High Commission, 35 Lowndes Square, London SW1X 9JN. TEl: (071) 235 2044.
Philippine Embassy, 199 Piccadilly, London W1V 9LE. Tel: (071) 493 9LE.
Singapore Embassy, 2 Wilton Crescent, London SW1X 8RW. Tel: (071) 235 8315.
Taiwan Embassy, 432-6 Grand Buidings, Trafalgar Square, London WC2 5HG. Tel: (071) 839 5901.
Thailand Embassy, 29-30 Queen's Gate, London SW7 5JB. Tel:

(071) 589 2944.
Vietnamese Embassy, 12-14 Victoria Road, London W8 5RD. Tel: (071) 937 1912/8564.

Overview

Asia is an area that is traditionally difficult for temporary workers to penetrate. Teaching English as a Foreign Language (TEFL) is a favourite standby for many travellers in Asia, and Japan is recognised as one of the best countries worldwide in which to ply this trade. Taiwan, Hong Kong and Korea are also rising fast in popularity with exponents of TEFL.

Although not officially sanctioned there are varied opportunities for the forward-thinking traveller: film extras, models, pineapple-sellers and a hostess in a karaoke bar. The capitalist nature of some Asian countries can be an advantage for people looking for work but you have to have an eye for the main chance.

Types of employment

Adventure companies

Exodus Expeditions, 9 Weir Road, London SW12 0LT. Tel: (081) 675 7996. Runs truck tours throughout Asia and adventure holidays in Nepal, Pakistan, India, Indonesia and China. Drivers and leaders need to have relevant experience and can expect to be on the road for 4-6 months.

Conservation

Earthwatch Europe, Belsyre Court, 57 Woodstock Road, Oxford OX2 6HU. Tel: (0865) 311600. Uses volunteers to support research work in fields ranging from archaeology to animal behaviour. Opeates throughout Asia and volunteers are expected to share the cost of the expedition. This can range from £500-£1200.

International Farm Experience Programme, YFC Centre, National Agricultural Centre, Stoneleigh Park, Kenilworth CV8 2LG. Tel: (0203) 696584. Provides placements for young farmers to work in China for 1-3 months. Applicants must be aged 18-26 and have at least two years' practical experience.

International Scientific Support Trust, 58 Battersea Park Road, London SW11 4JP. Tel: (071) 498 0855. Organises scientific and conservation projects to Indonesia. Participants must be over 18, and the cost of the expedition is about £2,500.

Project Barito Ulu, c/o Nicholas Morse, St Mary Hall, Belchamp Walter, Sudbury, Suffolk. Runs conservation projects in Borneo.

The Youth Charitable Organisation, 20-14 Urban Bank Street, PB 3, Yellamanchili, 531 055 Visakhapatnam DT, Andhra Pradesh, India. Uses volunteers for soil conservation work and general community development. Timescale of two weeks to six months.

Voluntary work

Much of the organised charity work that is available to the temporary worker is based in India. However, it must be taken into consideration that you cannot make much of an impact in a few days, or even weeks. People who want to do voluntary work in the Indian sub-continent should consider committing themselves for months rather than weeks.

Bombay Sarvodaya Friendship Centre, Friendship Building, Kajupada Pipe Line Road, Kurla, Bombay 400 072, India. Require volunteers for office or field work in rural or urban areas.

Committee for Coordination of Services of Displaced Persons in Thailand, 378B Soi 15, Petchburi Road, Bangkok, Thailand. Provide a list of various refugee work throughout south-east Asia.

Involvement Volunteers Association Inc., PO Box 218, Port Melbourne, Victoria 3207, Australia. Provide various volunteer placements, including a number in India.

Indian Volunteers for Community Service, 12 Eastleigh Avenue, South Harrow, Middlesex HA2 0UF. Uses volunteers for a rural development project in northern India.

Joint Assistance Centre, H-65, South Extension 1, New Delhi 110049, India. Require volunteers to provide disaster assistance in India. Volunteers are also required to teach English for three-month periods.

Missionaries of Charity, 54A A. J. C. Bose Road, Calcutta 16, India. Runs homes for orphaned children and the elderly. One of them is Mother Theresa's children's home in Calcutta (Shishu Bhavan, 78 Lower Circular Road).

Nava Dasrshanam, Gupta Towers, 3rd Floor, 50/1 Residence Road, Bangalore 560 025, India. Specialises in volunteers for organic farming.

Work camp organisations

Bangladesh Work Camp Association (BWCA), 289/2 Work Camps Road, North Shahjahanpur, Dhaka 17, Bangladesh. Runs work camps in rural and urban areas of Bangladesh.

HELP (SCOTLAND), 60 The Pleasance, Edinburgh EH8 9JT. Tel: (031) 556 9497. Runs work camps to help in the relief of poverty in various countries in Asia. The camps last for 4-6 weeks and there is no upper age limit.

NICE 401 Highhte Nishishinjuku 7-7-7, Tokyo 160, Japan. Organises work camps and conservation projects throughout Japan.

UNESCO Youth Centre, Korean National Commission for UNESCO, PO Box Central 64, Seoul, Korea 100. Organises work camps to promote international relations.

TEFL openings

Japan

With an estimated 9 million Japanese learning English at any one time it is not surprising that this is considered a prime area for TEFL teachers. While this is definitely still the case, competition has grown stiffer in recent years and the authorities and langauge schools are looking for well qualified teachers. Anyone with a degree and/or a recognised TEFL qualification should be able to find a teaching post in Japan. While the pay tends to be good – some travellers have earned in excess of £25 an hour – living costs are high and your employers will expect to get their money's worth.

Prospective TEFL teachers can check the advertisements in *Japan Times* or *Kansai Time Out* or even place their own. Another way to find work is to look up a number of language schools in the *Yellow Pages* and visit them in person. If you do this make sure that you are smartly dressed and you have all the relevant documents with you. The Japanese will pay great attention to your appearance. Once a job has been found a work permit should be obtained. Your employer will help you with this but a lot of workers do not bother and work illegally. The authorities have clamped down on this recently and illegal workers can face stiff fines if they are caught.

Some organisations who hire TEFL teachers to work in Japan:

Atty Language Institue, 5F Osaka Ekimae Daiichi Building 1-1-3 Umeda, Kita-ku, Osaka 530, Japan.

ECC Foreign Language Institute, Shikata Building 2F, 4-43 Nakazaki-Nishi, 2 chome, Kita-ku, Osaka 530, Japan.

International Education Services, Shin Talao Building, 10-7 Dogenzaka 2-chome, Shibuya-ku, Tokyo 150, Japan.

Nova Group, Knightsbridge House, 4th Floor, 197 Knightsbridge, London SW7 1RB. Tel: (071) 973 8866. Runs over 80 schools in Japan.

Saxoncourt (UK) Ltd, 59 South Molton Street, London W1Y 1HH. Tel: (071) 499 8533.

Other TEFL Opportunities
Hong Kong, Korea, Taiwan and Thailand have thriving TEFL industries but you should always keep an eye out for the less scrupulous operators. Scouring the local English newspapers is a good starting point and in some travellers have benefited from promoting their own talents in the affluent areas of cities in these countries. Useful addresses to contact include:

Hong Kong English Club, 1/F 190 Nathan Road, Kowloon, Hong Kong.

Anderson's Home and Corporate Department, 3rd Floor, 285 Fushing South Road, Sec. 1, Taipei, Taiwan. Hires English teachers to teach individuals in their homes or offices.

ELSI, 59 Chung King South Road, Section 2, Taipei, Taiwan. Runs language schools in Taipei and others parts of Taiwan.

GRAM English Institute, 7th Floor, 206 Tun Hwa South Road, Sec. 1, Taipei, Taiwan.

Hess, 51 Ho Ping East Road, Section 2, Taipei, Taiwan. Recruits teachers for children's classes.

American University Alumni Center, 179 Rajadamri Road, Bangkok 10330, Thailand.

Berlitz, 8 N. Satorn Road, Bangkok 10500, Thailand.

English and Computer College (ECC), 430/17-20 Chula Soi 64, Siam Square, Bangkok 10330, Thailand.

Inlingua School of Languages, 7th Floor, Central Chidlom Tower, 22 Ploenchit Road, Pathumwan, Bangkok 10330, Thailand.

TGD Co. Ltd, 28 Suhkumvit Soi 24, Bangkok 10110, Thailand.

Temporary job rating
Moderate. TEFL is a major industry in many Asian countries and the money is usually good. There are also other employment openings but you will have to be prepared to hustle a little bit and hope that the authorities do not catch up with you.

THE CARIBBEAN

Embassies
Antigua High Commission, 15 Thayer Street, London W1M 5LD. Tel: (071) 486 7073.

Bahamas High Commission, 10 Chesterfield Street, London W1X 8AH. Tel: (071) 499 0587.

Barbados High Commission, 1 Great Russell Street, London WC1B 3NH. Tel: (071) 631 4975.

Dominican Republic Embassy, 5 Braemar Mansions, Cornwall Gardens, London SW7 4AG. Tel: (071) 937 1921.

Jamaican High Commission, 1-2 Prince Consort Road, London SW7 2BZ. Tel: (071) 823 9911.

Trinidad and Tobago High Commission, 42 Belgrave Square, London SW1X 8NT. Tel: (071) 245 9351.

Overview

Naturally enough, considering its geographic location, the main source of casual employment is crewing on yachts that are sailing around the Caribbean or travelling to the USA. Experience is not always required but you will need to be persistent if you want to be taken on as a crew member on a small yacht. Officially you need to have working papers but if you hang around the harbours for long enough and display your willingness for hard work then the skippers may overlook this technicality.

There are also opportunities to work on passenger liners, who recruit through:

Greyhound Leisure, 8052 NW 14th St, Miami, FL 33126, USA.

Lawson Marine Services Limited, Royal House, 2 Palmyra Place, Newport, Gwent NP9 4EJ.

Stella Cruise Services, 333 Biscayne Blvd., Miami, FL 33132, USA.

Travelmate, 6 Hayes Avenue, Bournemouth BH7 7AD. Recruits a variety of staff including bar staff, kitchen staff, waiting staff, photographers and entertainers.

Windjammer Barefoot Cruises, Box 120, Miami Beach, FL 33139, USA. Tel: (305) 672 6453.

BUNAC also operates a Work Jamaica programme (see Chapter 4).

Temporary work rating

Moderate – if you yearn for a life on the ocean waves then the Caribbean could be the plce for you. There are also a small number of voluntary jobs available through organisations in the UK and the occasional au pair position. If you do work on a yacht or a cruise ship then you may make some useful contacts to enable you to pick up a job when you get back to dry land.

6
The Final Edge

CASE HISTORIES

Newly weds on working holiday honeymoon

Paul and Kath Downie spent their honeymoon on a working holiday in Europe. As Paul noted, it was an experience they will not forget in a hurry.

'Our first stop was in Greece and Kath soon found work in a restaurant on Kos. I spent a bit of time in one of the local bars and through this I met the captain of a luxury yacht belonging to a millionaire. He offered me a job as a chef and I spent the next months cruising around the Greek islands cooking for millionaires! The pay was good — about £200 a week — and our quarters were luxurious as far as I was concerned. When we went ashore we were sent shopping and told to buy about £2000 worth of food and whatever we wanted for ourselves.

The work itself was just a case of preparing lunch and dinner and although it was hard work at times it was well worth it to see how the other half lived. However, not all people on luxury yachts were so lucky and we met some who had to work extremely long hours for cantankerous bosses and they lived in very cramped conditions.

After Greece we went to Austria but we were unable to find work because both the employment services and prospective employers would not consider anyone who could not speak German.'

A model worker in Japan

Sarah Hunter arrived in Singapore with the intention of teaching English but ended up working as a model.

'There are several modelling agencies in Singapore and as long as you avoid the seedier looking ones you should be able to find reputable modelling work. There is a certain amount of competition but you do not have to look like Naomi Campbell or Chrissie Brinkley in order to land jobs. As long as you are smart and presentable you should have a chance. I modelled a variety of items, from hats to sunglasses. The working day was sometimes long, up to ten hours, a lot of which is standing around waiting, but on average I earned £180 for a week's work.'

Keeping safe in South Africa

Guy Crichton arrived in South Africa with just one contact and he was soon working as a burglar alarm salesman.

'While I was travelling through Zimbabwe I stayed with a friend who gave me the address of his brother in Durban. When I met him we got on really well and after a week he offered me a job as a door-to-door salesman for his security company. He was totally unconcerned about my lack of work permit and I was even paid through the books. The job was a typical sales job and although I had my fair share of doors slammed in my face I also met a lot of interesting people. I left South Africa at the beginning of 1993 as the employment situation was deteriorating in all sectors of the economy. I think I may have been lucky to get in when I did because it seemed as if unemployment was going to rise considerably.'

Skiing to success Down Under

Stuart Markham, travelling with a working holiday visa, was surprised at his first job in Australia.

'I didn't even know they had snow in Australia but when I visited the Snowy Mountains I discovered that there was more snow than in the European Alps. I popped into the CES in Thredbo and immediately saw an advertisement for a ski instructor for teenagers. My skiing ability was average but I managed to bluff my way to a certain extent and ended up spending six weeks teaching 13-year-olds to stay upright on the snow. I think workers in Australia should give the ski resorts more consideration because they tend to be a bit of a neglected area. While I was there I met a lot of other travellers who were working in bars, hotels and chalets which made for a very active social life as well.'

The dishwasher's story

Kay Murray left her job as a shop assistant and spent two months playing with European soapsuds.

'When I started looking for work abroad I decided that the most easily available type of work would be dishwashing because it was so dirty and gruelling. I was right on both counts! It was relatively easy to find jobs and I scrubbed my way through France, Italy and Greece. The work was uniformly grotty and tiring and kitchens are not always the most sociable of places. But I usually made over £120 a week and as many potato peelings as I could eat. But after six weeks I decided that enough was enough and graduated to being a waitress in a Greek taverna. If you want to make money and have a high boredom threshold then dishwashing is one option that should be kept in mind.'

The ups and downs of BUNAC

Catherine Smyllie worked as a sports instructor at a BUNAC camp in Vermont.

'It was undoubtedly the hardest two months work that I have ever done. It was non-stop from morning to night and the kids seemed to think that you should have as much energy as they did — and be on call 24 hours a day. Although they were very demanding they ensured that there was never a dull moment! The best thing about the camp was the other counsellors and they provided a bit of welcome relief from the strains of the work. After the camp I spent a month travelling around New England with two of the other counsellors.'

On the move after half a century

Mary Cole left for Italy on her fiftieth birthday, armed only with a TEFL qualification and an optimistic attitude.

'My first port of call was Florence and my first job was cleaning the houses of some of the better-off citizens of the city. This helped me get a few contacts and although I could not find any work at the language schools in Florence I soon had a network of private students. I supplemented this with teaching a couple of nightclasses a week. I don't think my age was a disadvantage and in many ways it was a benefit because the students seemed to have more confidence in older people because they believed they are more experienced. It was a pretty precarious existence at times but a marvellous way to get to know the country and its people.'

A life under canvas

John Livingstone worked in France for one of the top camping companies and there was never a dull moment.

'I was employed as a member of the flying squad. This meant that we had to work in the company's warehouse and load hundreds of tents into lorries. They were then delivered to the camp sites where other flying squads erected them. Our job was to travel around all the camp sites, ironing out problems and delivering any equipment that had been forgotten. Over the course of two months we visited over 50 sites around France and did everything from rewiring fridges to digging trenches. The great advantage to me of being in the flying squad was that you did not have to be able to speak French — although I had picked up quite a bit by the time I had finished.'

7
Useful Addresses

GENERAL

Archaeology Abroad, 31/34 Gordon Square, London WC1H 0PY.

British Council, 65 Davis Street, London W1Y 2AA. Tel: (071) 930 8466.

British Universities North America Club (BUNAC), 16 Bowling Green Lane, London EC1R 0BD. Tel: (071) 630 0344.

Camp America, 37a Queen's Gate, London SW7 5HR. Tel: (071) 589 3223.

Careers Research and Advisory Centre (CRAC), Bateman Street, Cambridge CB2 1LZ.

Cavendish Educational Consultants, 22 Hills Road, Cambridge CB2 1JP. Tel: (0223) 69483.

Central Bureau for Educational Visits and Exchanges, Seymour Mews House, Seymour Mews, London W1H 9PE. Tel: (071) 486 5101. A wealth of information and literature covering a wide range of opportunities for working abroad.

Concordia Youth Service Volunteers, 8 Brunswick Place, Hove, East Sussex BN3 1ET. Tel: (0273) 772086.

Coordinating Committee For International Voluntary Service, UNESCO – 1 rue Miollis, 75015 Paris, France. Tel: 4568 27 31.

Intercultural Educational Programme (IEP), 33 Seymour Place, London W1H 5AP. Tel: (071) 402 3305.

International Voluntary Service (IVS), 162 Upper New Walk, Leicester LE1 7QA. Tel: (0533) 549430.

Jobs in the Alps, PO Box 388, London SW1X 8LX.

Kibbutz Representatives, 1A Accommodation Road, London NW11. Tel: (081) 458 9235.

Overseas Job Express, PO Box 22, Brighton BN1 6HX. Tel: (0273) 440220.

Project 67, 10 Hatton Garden, London EC1N 8AH. Tel: (071) 831 7626.

Trailfinders, 42–50 Earls Court Road, London W8 6EJ. Tel: (071) 938 3366.

Travel Trade Gazette Directory, PO Box 20, Sovereign Way, Tonbridge, Kent TN9 1RQ.

Vacation Work, 9 Park End Street, Oxford OX1 1HJ. Tel: (0865) 241978.

Voluntary Service Overseas (VSO), 317 Putney Bridge Road, London SW15 2PN. Tel: (081) 780 2266.

Volunteer Centre, 29 Lower King's Road, Berkhamstead, Herts HP4 2AE.

WEXAS International Ltd, 45–49 Brompton Road, London SW3 1DE.

Youth Hostel Association, Trevelyan House, 8 St Stephen's Hill, St Albans, Herts AL1 2DY. Tel: (0727) 55215.

HEALTH

British Airways Immunization Centre, 156 Regent Street, London W1. Tel: (071) 439 9584.

Department of Infections and Tropical Medicine, East Birmingham Hospital, Bordesley Green East, Birmingham B9 5ST. Tel: (021) 766 6611.

Hospital for Tropical Diseases, 4 St Pancras Way, London NW1 0PE. Tel: (071) 387 4411 or (071) 388 8989/9600 (travel clinic) or (0898) 345 081 (pre-recorded healthline).

Department of Infection and Tropical Medicine, Ruchill Hospital, Glasgow G20 9NB. Tel: (041) 946 7120.

8
Further Reading

EMPLOYMENT

Applying for a United States Visa, Richard Fleischer (International Venture Handbooks, Plymbridge Distributors Ltd, Plymouth, 1993). Tel: (0752) 695745.
The Au Pair and Nanny's Guide to Working Abroad (Vacation Work).
Directory of Jobs and Careers Abroad (Vacation Work).
Directory of Work and Study in Developing Countries (Vacation Work).
Home From Home (Central Bureau).
How to Emigrate, Roger Jones (How To Books, 1994).
How to Get a Job Abroad, Roger Jones (How To Books, 3rd edition, 1994).
How to Get a Job in America, Roger Jones (How To Books, 2nd edition, 1994).
How to Get a Job in Australia, Nick Vandome (How To Books, 1992).
How to Get a Job in Europe, Mark Hempshell (How To Books, 2nd edition, 1994).
How to Get a Job in France, Mark Hempshell (How To Books, 1993).
How to Live & Work in America, Steve Mills, (How To Books, 2nd edition, 1992).
How to Live & Work in Australia, Laura Veltman (How To Books, 4th edition, 1994).
How to Live & Work in Belgium, Marvina Shilling (How To Books, 1991).
How to Live & Work in France, Marie Prevost Logan (How To Books, 2nd edition, 1993).

How to Live & Work in Germany, Nessa Loewenthal (How To Books, 1991).

How to Live & Work in Hong Kong, Martin Bennett (How To Books, 1992).

How to Live & Work in Italy, Amanda Hinton (How To Books, 1993).

How to Live & Work in Japan, Aaron Hoopes (How To Books, 1992).

How to Live & Work in New Zealand, Joy Muirhead (How To Books, 1994).

How to Live & Work in Portugal, Sue Tyson-Ward (How To Books, 1993).

How to Live & Work in Saudi Arabia, Joy McGregor & Margaret Nydell (How To Books, 1991).

How To Live & Work in Spain, Robert A C Richards (How To Books, 1992).

How To Spend a Year Abroad, Nick Vandome (How To Books, 1992).

How to Study Abroad, Teresa Tinsley (How To Books 2nd edition, 1994).

How to Teach Abroad, Roger Jones (How To Books 2nd edition 1994).

International Directory of Voluntary Work (Vacation Work).

Jobs in Japan (Vacation Work).

Kibbutz Volunteer (Vacation Work).

Overseas Jobs Express, PO Box 22, Brighton BN1 6HX. Fortnightly newspaper containing numerous job vacancies and information for expats.

The Student Handbook, (Macmillan Publishers Ltd, 4 Little Essex Street, London WC2R 3LF).

Summer Jobs Abroad (Vacation Work).

Volunteer Work (Central Bureau).

Work Your Way Around the World (Vacation Work).

Working Abroad: Essential Advice for Expatriates and their Employers, Jonathan Golding (International Venture Handbooks, Plymbridge Distributors Ltd, Plymouth, 1993). Tel: (0752) 695745.

Working Holidays (Central Bureau).

Working in Europe (Department of Employment — free).

Working in the European Communities (CRAC).

The Working Traveller, Compass House, Horsecroft Road, The Pinnacles, Harlow, Essex CM19 5BN. Tel: (0279) 411105.

TRAVEL

The Budget Travel Handbook (Horizon, Plymbridge House, Estover Road, Plymouth PL6 7PZ).
An Explorer's Handbook (Hodder & Stoughton, 47 Bedford Square, London WC1B 3DP).
Handbook for Women Travellers (Piatkus, 5 Windmill Street, London W1P 1HF).
Lonely Planet Guides, PO Box 617, Hawthorn, Victoria 3122, Australia.
Nothing Ventured — Disabled People Travel the World (Rough Guide).
Overseas Timetable — Railway, Road and Shipping (Thomas Cook).
Rough Guides (Harrap-Columbus).
The Traveller's Handbook (WEXAS).
Women Travel (Rough Guide, Harrap-Columbus, Chelsea House, 26 Market Square, Bromley, Kent BR1 1NA).

HEALTH

Traveller's Health: How to Stay Healthy Abroad (OUP, Walton Street, Oxford OX2 6DP).
The Traveller's Health Guide (Lascelles, 47 York Road, Brentford, Middlesex TW8 0QP).

Index

Addresses, 151-152
Adventure travel companies, 43-44, 139, 142
Africa, 138-141
AIDS, 23
Algeria, 138
Antigua, 145
Argentina, 135
Asia, 141-145
Au pair, 65
Australia, 117-127
Austria, 70-71

Bahamas, 145
Bangladesh, 141
Barbados, 145
Belgium, 71-74
Belize, 135
Benefits, 12
Bolivia, 135
Bradt Publications, 30
Brazil, 135
British Council, 35, 50
Bulgaria, 74-75
BUNAC, 61-65
Bunacamp, 62-63

Cadogan Guides, 29
Canada, 133-135
Camp America, 65
Camping firms, 44-45
Caribbean, 145-146
Certificates, 25
Chile, 135-136
China, 141
Clothes, 25
Conservation, 137, 139, 142-143
Costa Rica, 135
Couriers, 45-46
Cuba, 135
CV, 36-38
Cyprus, 75
Czech Republic, 75-76

Denmark, 76-79
Department of Social Security Overseas Branch, 24-25
Dominican Republic, 146
Driving, 34

Ecuador, 135
Egypt, 138
Europe, 67-117

Finland, 79-80
Flying squad, 46
Fodor Guides, 30
France, 80-90
Further reading, 153-155

Germany, 90-94
Graduates, 10
Greece, 94-96
Guidebooks, 28-31

Health, 21-24, 152
Heritage, 14
Hong Kong, 141
Hospitality industry, 33
How To Books, 29
Hungary, 96-97

Iceland, 97
India, 141, 143
Indonesia, 141
Insurance, 20-21
International Reply Coupon, 35
Israel, 127-130
Italy, 97-99

Jamaica, 146
Japan, 141, 144
Job experience, 33-35
Job hunting, 25-26

KAMP, 63
Kenya, 138
Kibbutz, 128-129
Korea, 141

Language courses, 40-41
Lesotho, 138
Let's Go Guides, 30
Letters, 25
Long-term unemployed, 11
Lonely Planet Guides, 29
Luxembourg, 99-102

Malawi, 138
Malaysia, 141
Malta, 102
Medical bag, 23-24
Medical treatment, 24-25
Mexico, 135-137
Money, 14-15
Morocco, 138
Moshavim, 129
Motivation, 16-17
Murphy's Law, 15

National Vacancy System, 67
Nepal, 141
Netherlands, 102-105
New Zealand, 127
Newspapers, 31-32
Nicaragua, 135
Nigeria, 138
North America, 130-135
Norway, 105-106

Overseas Job Express, 67

Pakistan, 141
Paraguay, 135
Passport, 18
Passport offices, 18-19
Peru, 135
Philippines, 141
Pocket guidebooks, 30-31
Poland, 106-107
Portugal, 107-108

Recession, 15
Redundancy, 10
References, 25, 38
Romania, 109
Rough Guides, 29

School leavers, 9
Short-term break, 11
Sierra Leone, 138
Singapore, 141
Ski companies, 46-47
Spain, 109-113

South Africa, 138
South and Central America, 135-138
Students, 10
Summer schools, 34-35
Sweden, 113-114
Switzerland, 114-116

Taiwan, 141
Tanzania, 138
Teaching English as a Foreign Language (TEFL), 34-35, 47-51, 136-137, 139, 144-145
TEFL qualifications, 48
Thailand, 141
Training Access Points, 40
Translation, 41-42
Travel and Trade Publications, 30
Travel writing, 31
Trinidad and Tobago, 146
Tunisia, 138
Turkey, 116-117

Unemployment, 11
United States of America, 130-133

Vacation Work Publications, 30
Vaccinations, 22
Vietnam, 142
Visas, 19
Voluntary organisations, 51-60
Voluntary work, 33-34, 138, 143

Work America, 63-64
Work Australia, 64
Work Canada, 64
Work camps, 60-61, 140-141, 143-144
Work experience, 12-13
Work Jamaica, 64
Work Malta, 64
Working holiday, 11-12

Youth organisations, 61-65
Zaire, 139
Zimbabwe, 139

Other books in this series

How to Get a Job Abroad
Roger Jones

This top-selling title is essential for everyone planning to spend a period abroad. It contains a big reference section of medium and long-term job opportunities and possibilities, arranged by region and country of the world, and by profession/occupation. There are more than 130 pages of specific contacts and leads, giving literally hundreds of addresses and much hard-to-find information. There is a classified guide to overseas recruitment agencies, and even a multi-lingual guide to writing application letters. 'A fine book for anyone considering even a temporary overseas job.' *The Evening Star*. 'A highly informative and well researched book. . . containing lots of hard information and a first class reference section. . . A superb buy.' *The Escape Committee Newsletter*. 'A valuable addition to any careers library.' *Phoenix (Association of Graduate Careers Advisory Services)*. 'An excellent addition to any careers library . . . Compact and realistic. . . There is a wide range of reference addresses covering employment agencies, specialist newspapers, a comprehensive booklist and helpful addresses . . . All readers, whether careers officers, young adults or more mature adults, will find use for this book.' *Newscheck/Careers Services Bulletin.*

272pp illus. 1 85703 115 6. 3rd edition.

How to Get a Job in Europe
Mark Hempshell

The Single European Market and Europe's rise as the world's leading economic unit, has made it *the* place to get a job. This new **How To** book is the first to set out exactly what opportunities exist in Europe. It contains step-by-step guidance on how to find the vacancies, how to apply, and how to understand and adapt to the cultural and legal framework. Packed throughout with key contacts, sample documents and much hard-to-find information, this book will be an absolutely essential starting point for everyone job-hunting in Europe, whether as a school or college leaver, graduate trainee, technician or professional — and indeed anyone wanting to live and work as a European whether for just a summer vacation or on a more permanent basis. 'I learned a lot from the book and was impressed at the amount of information it contained.' *Newscheck/Careers Service Bulletin.* Mark Hempshell is a freelance writer who specialises in writing on overseas employment.

208pp illus. 1 85703 128 8. 2nd edition.